U0092757

學科能力測驗、指定科目考試、全民英檢中級適用

英語 *Make Me High* 系列

學測指考英文

英文 致勝句型

附隨堂評量

王隆興 編著

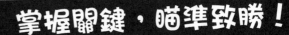

掌握關鍵，瞄準致勝！

關鍵 **1** 名師嚴選80個句型重點！

完整收錄大考常見句型，並比較易混淆的句型，清楚掌握重點，舉一反三。

關鍵 **2** 解說清楚明瞭一看就懂！

重點一目瞭然，說明淺顯易懂好吸收，考前衝刺神隊友，迅速提升考場即戰力。

關鍵 **3** 隨堂評量實戰練習現學現用！

隨書附贈20回隨堂評量，及時檢視學習成果、熟悉句型，以收事半功倍之效。

三民書局

國家圖書館出版品預行編目資料

學測指考英文致勝句型／王隆興編著.－－初版一刷.－－臺北市: 三民, 2019
　　　面；　公分

ISBN 978–957–14–6512–8　（平裝）
1. 英語教學 2. 句法 3. 中等教育

524.38　　　　　　　　　　　　　　　107019147

© 學測指考英文致勝句型

編 著 者	王隆興
責任編輯	王雅瑩　范榮約
美術編輯	郭雅萍
發 行 人	劉振強
著作財產權人	三民書局股份有限公司
發 行 所	三民書局股份有限公司
	地址　臺北市復興北路386號
	電話　(02)25006600
	郵撥帳號　0009998–5
門 市 部	(復北店)臺北市復興北路386號
	(重南店)臺北市重慶南路一段61號
出版日期	初版一刷　2019年3月
編　　號	S 805910

行政院新聞局登記證局版臺業字第〇二〇〇號

有著作權‧不准侵害

ISBN　978–957–14–6512–8　（平裝）

序

英語 Make Me High 系列的理想在於超越，在於創新。

這是時代的精神，也是我們出版的動力；

這是教育的目的，也是我們進步的執著。

針對英語的全球化與未來的升學趨勢，

我們設計了一系列適合普高、技高學生的英語學習書籍。

面對英語，不會徬徨不再迷惘，學習的心徹底沸騰，

心情好 High！

實戰模擬，掌握先機知己知彼，百戰不殆決勝未來，

分數更 High！

選擇優質的英語學習書籍，才能激發學習的強烈動機；

興趣盎然便不會畏懼艱難，自信心要自己大聲說出來。

本書如良師指引循循善誘，如益友相互鼓勵攜手成長。

展書輕閱，你將發現……

學習英語原來也可以這麼 High！

給讀者的話

　　本書《學測指考英文致勝句型》意在用淺顯易懂的文字與例句，將大考易考的句型做一有系統的整理與解說。冀望同學在學得這些句型後，能在閱讀能力上有所提升，且在書寫作文時，也能將這些實用句型運用在其中，為文章增添色彩 (add color to the composition)。本書在每一單元中，盡可能用簡單精確的文字，將複雜的文法做一深入淺出的說明。除了可當老師輔助教本外，讀者也可拿來做自我學習使用。每一單元最後都附有練習題，並在書末提供解答；同時還另外附贈「隨堂評量」夾冊，以作為讀者自我檢測學習成效之用。

　　本書分 12 章，80 個單元。將大考常出現且同學常易混淆的句型分在同一章，以便同學對照學習。例如第 1 章第 1 單元介紹動詞，將 [連綴動詞]、[感官動詞]、[使役動詞] 做一詳細的解說。方便同學比較其差異與學習，以達事半功倍之效。在第 13 單元完成式的句型中，大考也出現多次這種句型的翻譯。其餘各單元與句型，也都是在學習英文的過程中，必須熟知的必備知識。期望同學能詳讀本書中的各章節，相信對大考一定助益良多。本書所列的很多句型也都可套用在大考作文上。例如第 11 章第 71 單元的 It can't be denied that... 句型，用在作文中能使文章更通順。相關句型不勝枚舉，筆者不再一一羅列。唯望讀者能親自熟讀，必當能體會本書之妙用。

　　欣見本書順利付梓，但實非筆者一人之力所能為，十分感謝三民書局編輯部同仁傾力協助。另，筆者才疏學淺，疏漏之處在所難免，望先進不吝指正。

王隆興
於臺北市立南港高級中學

Table of Contents

Chapter 1　動詞相關句型

單元 1　S + { look; sound; taste; smell; / feel; seem; appear; prove; + adj. / stay/keep/remain; turn/become/get/grow } ... 01

單元 2　S + { see/watch/look at; / hear/listen to; + O + OC (V-ing/V/p.p.) / feel/observe } ... 02

單元 3　S + find/keep/leave + O + OC (adj./V-ing/p.p.) ... 04

單元 4　S (人) + spend + time/money + { V-ing / on + N }
{ S (物) + cost + O (人) + money... / It cost(s) + O (人) + money + to V... }
{ It takes + O (人) + time + to V... / S (人) + take + time + to V... }
S (人) + take one's time + V-ing ... 05

單元 5　S + { cannot help but + V / cannot help + V-ing / have no choice but + to V } ... 06

單元 6　S (人) + used to + V
S (人) + { be / get } used to + { V-ing / N } ... 07

單元 7　S + { would rather + V_1...than + V_2... / prefer + V_1-ing/N... + to + V_2-ing/N... / prefer to + V_1...rather than + V_2... } ... 08

單元 8　{ S + consider + sb./sth. + (to be) + N/adj. / S + { see/view/regard/think of/ / look (up)on/take/perceive } + sb./sth. + as + N/adj. }
S + refer to + sb./sth. + as + N/adj.
S + recognize + sb./sth. + as + N/adj. ... 09

單元 9　S (人) + { inform; remind; convince; / rob; deprive; accuse; + sb. + of + N... / relieve; cure } ... 10

| 單元 10 | A + $\left\{\begin{array}{l}\text{comprise}\\ \text{consist of}\\ \text{be comprised/composed of}\\ \text{be made up of}\end{array}\right\}$ + B | 11 |

| 單元 11 | S + $\left\{\begin{array}{l}\text{be + located/situated...}\\ \text{stand/sit/lie...}\end{array}\right.$ | 12 |

| 單元 12 | S + happen (+ to sb.)...
S + occur... | 13 |

Chapter 2　助動詞相關句型

| 單元 13 | S + have/has + p.p. $\left\{\begin{array}{l}\text{+ for + 一段時間}\\ \text{+ since + 過去式子句 (+ 一段時間 + ago)}\\ \text{+ since + 年代／季節／月分}\\ \text{+ so far}\\ \text{+ over the past years/in recent years}\\ \text{+ for a long time/for ages}\end{array}\right.$ | 15 |

| 單元 14 | By the time + S + V-ed..., S + had + p.p.
By the time + S + V..., S will have + p.p. | 16 |

| 單元 15 | S + $\left\{\begin{array}{l}\text{must + V}\\ \text{must + have + p.p.}\end{array}\right.$ | 17 |

| 單元 16 | S + $\left\{\begin{array}{l}\text{suggest; recommend;}\\ \text{advise; insist;}\\ \text{request; demand, require;}\\ \text{command, order}\end{array}\right\}$ + that + S (+ should) + V | 18 |

| 單元 17 | S + V_1... + $\left\{\begin{array}{l}\text{for fear of + N/}V_2\text{-ing...}\\ \text{for fear that + S + would/will/might/may + }V_2...\\ \text{lest + S (+ should) + }V_2...\end{array}\right.$ | 19 |

Chapter 3　動狀詞相關句型

| 單元 18 | $\left\{\begin{array}{l}\text{To/In order to + }V_1..., \text{S + }V_2...\\ \text{S + }V_2... \text{+ to/in order to + }V_1...\end{array}\right.$ | 20 |

| 單元 19 | To V_1/V_1-ing... + V_2... | 21 |

單元 20	S + have + { trouble/difficulty/ a hard time/problems } + (in) V-ing	23
單元 21	There is no + V-ing...	24
單元 22	V_1-ing/p.p...., S + V_2...　(分詞構句)	25
單元 23	{ With + NP, S + V... S + V...(,) with + O + OC }　(表狀態)	27
單元 24	S + V, { including... ...included inclusive of... }	28

Chapter 4　代名詞相關句型

單元 25	{ one...the other... one...another...the other... } { one...another... one...another...still another... } { some of...the others... some...others... some...others...still others... }	30
單元 26	someone, somebody; something; anyone; anything; nobody; nothing } + adj.	31
單元 27	S + have + { a lot/much something a little little nothing } + to do with...	32

Chapter 5　形容詞與副詞相關句型

單元 28	be + adj. = be + of + N	34
單元 29	{ (Much) to the N of sb., S + V... (Much) to one's N, S + V... }	34
單元 30	{ a lot/much/far slightly/a little/a bit even/still } + 比較級	36

單元 31	The more + S + V$_1$..., the more + S + V$_2$... The + 比較級 + S + V$_1$..., the + 比較級 + S + V$_2$...	37
單元 32	S$_1$ + V$_1$ + 倍數 + $\begin{cases} \text{as + adj./adv. + as + S}_2\ (+ V_2) \\ \text{比較級 + than + S}_2\ (+ V_2) \\ \text{the N of + S}_2 \end{cases}$	38
單元 33	S$_1$ + V$_1$ + $\begin{cases} \text{as/so + adj./adv. + as} \\ \text{as many + N + as} \\ \text{as much + N + as} \end{cases}$ + S$_2$ (+ V$_2$)	39
單元 34	S + V + as + adj./adv. + as + $\begin{cases} \text{possible} \\ \text{sb. can} \end{cases}$	40

Chapter 6 介系詞相關句型

單元 35	look forward to be/get used to devote sth./yourself to + N/V-ing What do you say to be opposed to/object to	41
單元 36	prevent/stop/keep/ prohibit/bar/deter + N + from + N/V-ing	42
單元 37	be + $\begin{cases} \text{famous/noted/known/} \\ \text{well-known/renowned} \end{cases}$ + for/as...	43
單元 38	be addicted to + N/V-ing indulge in + N/V-ing	44
單元 39	Instead of + N/V$_1$-ing..., S + V$_2$... Rather than + N/V$_1$-ing/V$_1$..., S + V$_2$... S + V$_2$...instead of + N/V$_1$-ing... S + V$_2$...rather than + N/V$_1$-ing/V$_1$... S + V$_1$...; instead, S + V$_2$... S + V$_1$.... Instead/Rather, S + V$_2$... S + V$_1$...; S + V$_2$...instead.	45
單元 40	lead to/contribute to/give rise to result in/bring about	47

Chapter 7 連接詞相關句型

單元 41	$S_1 + \begin{cases} \text{be..., and so + be} \\ \text{aux...., and so + aux.} \\ \text{V..., and so + do/does/did} \end{cases} + S_2$	48
單元 42	or, otherwise unless	49
單元 43	$\begin{cases} \text{neither A nor B} \\ \text{either A or B} \\ \text{A as well as B} \\ \text{both A and B} \\ \text{not only A (but) also B} \end{cases}$	50
單元 44	$\begin{cases} \text{As soon as + S + V...} \\ \text{The moment/instant/minute (that) + S + V...} \\ \text{Upon/On V-ing...} \\ \text{No sooner had + S + p.p....than + S + V-ed...} \end{cases}$	51
單元 45	$S + V_1 + \underline{\text{so that/in order that}} + S + \text{aux.} + V_2$	52
單元 46	$\begin{cases} \text{Whether... (or not), S + V} \\ \text{Whether...or..., S + V} \\ \text{Whether + S + } V_1 \text{ (or not) + be/}V_2... \\ \text{S + V + \underline{whether/if}... (or not)} \end{cases}$	53
單元 47	$\begin{cases} \underline{\text{Although/Though}} + S + V_1, S + V_2... \\ \underline{\text{Despite/In spite of}} + \text{the fact that} + S + V_1, S + V_2... \\ \underline{\text{Despite/In spite of/Notwithstanding}} + N/V_1\text{-ing}, S + V_2... \end{cases}$	55
單元 48	$\begin{cases} \text{(As) adj./adv. as} + S + V_1..., S + V_2... \\ \text{Although} + S + V_1..., S + V_2... \end{cases}$	56
單元 49	$\begin{cases} \text{While} + S + V_1, S + V_2... \\ S + V_2...\text{while} + S + V_1... \end{cases}$	57
單元 50	$\begin{cases} \text{Because} + S + V_1..., S + V_2... \\ \begin{cases} \underline{\text{Because of/As a result of/}} \\ \underline{\text{Owing to/Due to}} \end{cases} + N/V\text{-ing}, S + V... \end{cases}$	58
單元 51	$\begin{cases} \underline{\text{Because/Since}} + S + V_1..., S + V_2... \\ S + V_2...\underline{\text{because/since/for}} + S + V_1... \end{cases}$	59

Chapter 8　關係代名詞、副詞與名詞子句相關句型

單元 52　S + V₁..., 數量詞 + of whom/which + V₂... — 61

單元 53　$\begin{cases} \text{What} \\ \text{All (that)} \end{cases}$ + S + have/need to do is (to) + V... — 62

單元 54　$\begin{cases} \text{...whoever...} \\ \text{...whomever...} \\ \text{...whichever...} \\ \text{...whatever...} \end{cases}$ + (S) + V... — 63

單元 55　S + V + $\begin{cases} \text{the very} \\ \text{the only} \\ \text{the same} \end{cases}$ + N + that... — 64

單元 56　The idea/fact/belief/thought that S + V₁... + V₂...
S + V₁ + the idea/fact/belief/thought that S + V₂... — 65

單元 57　...wh- + S + V　　(名詞子句) — 66

Chapter 9　虛主詞與虛受詞相關句型

單元 58　It + $\begin{cases} \text{occurs to sb.} \\ \text{strikes sb.} \\ \text{dawns on sb.} \end{cases}$ + that + S + V... — 68

單元 59　$\begin{cases} \text{It is not surprising that + S + V...} \\ \text{It comes as no surprise that + S + V...} \\ \text{Unsurprisingly, S + V...} \end{cases}$ — 69

單元 60　$\begin{cases} \text{It is likely that + S + V...} \\ \text{S + be likely to + V...} \end{cases}$ — 70

單元 61　It is + $\begin{cases} \text{important/vital/} \\ \text{crucial/critical/} \\ \text{necessary/essential} \end{cases}$ + that + S + (should) + V — 71

單元 62　$\begin{cases} \text{It seems/seemed that + S + V} \\ \text{S + seem/seemed to +} \begin{cases} \text{V} \\ \text{have + p.p.} \end{cases} \end{cases}$ — 72

| 單元 63 | $\begin{cases} \text{It is + adj. + for sb. + to V} \\ \text{To V + is + adj. + for sb.} \\ \text{V-ing + is + adj. + for sb.} \end{cases}$ | 73 |

| 單元 64 | Rumor/Legend has it that + S + V... | 74 |

| 單元 65 | S + $\begin{cases} \text{make/find} \\ \text{consider/think} \end{cases}$ + it + adj./N + (for sb.) + to V | 75 |

Chapter 10　假設用法相關句型

| 單元 66 | If + S + were/V-ed..., S + would/might/could/should + V...
If + S + had + p.p...., S + would/might/could/should + have + p.p.... | 76 |

| 單元 67 | $\begin{cases} \text{If it were not for + N, S + could/might/would/should + V} \\ \text{Were it not for + N, S + could/might/would/should + V} \\ \text{If it had not been for + N, S + could/might/would/should + have + p.p.} \\ \text{Had it not been for + N, S + could/might/would/should + have + p.p.} \end{cases}$ | 77 |

| 單元 68 | S + wish + (that) + 子句
S + wish + O + N...
S + wish + to V... | 78 |

| 單元 69 | $\begin{cases} \text{It's (high) time + for sb. + to V...} \\ \text{It's (high) time + that + S + V-ed...} \end{cases}$ | 79 |

Chapter 11　否定用法相關句型

| 單元 70 | S + $\begin{cases} \text{no} \\ \text{not} \\ \text{never} \end{cases}$ + V_1 + without + N/V_2-ing | 81 |

| 單元 71 | $\begin{cases} \text{It can't be denied that + S + V...} \\ \text{There is no denying that + S + V...} \\ \text{No one can deny that + S + V...} \end{cases}$ | 82 |

| 單元 72 | S + cannot/can't/can never + $\begin{cases} \text{be + too + adj.} \\ \text{V (+ O) + too + adv.} \end{cases}$ | 83 |

| 單元 73 | S + V_1..., $\begin{cases} \text{not to mention} \\ \text{not to speak of} \\ \text{to say nothing of} \end{cases}$ + V_2-ing...
S + V_1..., $\begin{cases} \text{let alone} \\ \text{much less} \end{cases}$ + V_2... | 84 |

Chapter 12　特殊句構相關句型

單元 74	Not only + $\begin{cases} \text{aux.} + S + V... \\ \text{be} + S... \end{cases}$, but + S + $\begin{cases} \text{also} + V \\ \text{be...also...} \\ \text{aux.} + \text{also} + V... \end{cases}$ Not until... + aux. + S + V...	86
單元 75	地方副詞 + 代名詞 + 動詞 地方副詞 + 動詞 + 名詞	87
單元 76	$\begin{cases} S + V + \text{only if} + S + V \\ \text{Only if} + S + V + \text{aux.} + S + V \\ S + V + \text{only when} + S + V \\ \text{Only when} + S + V + \text{aux.} + S + V \end{cases}$	88
單元 77	What + (a/an) + adj. + N (+ S + V)! How + adj. (+ S + V)!	89
單元 78	It is/was + N + that...	90
單元 79	$\begin{cases} S + \text{aux.} + \text{not} + V...\text{until}... \\ \text{Not until}... + \text{aux.} + S + V... \\ \text{It is/was not until}... + \text{that} + S + V... \end{cases}$	91
單元 80	分數的寫法 1/3: one-third 2/5: two-fifths 137/217: one hundred and thirty seven over two hundred and seventeen	92

Answer Key 94

略語表

略語	中英文名稱	略語	中英文名稱
adj.	adjective（形容詞）	p.p.	past participle（過去分詞）
adv.	adverb（副詞）	prep.	preposition（介系詞）
aux.	auxiliary（助動詞）	S	Subject（主詞）
conj.	conjunction（連接詞）	SC	Subject Complement（主詞補語）
DO	Direct Object（直接受詞）	V	verb（動詞）
IO	Indirect Object（間接受詞）	V-ed	past tense（過去式）
N	noun（名詞）	V-ing	gerund（動名詞）
NP	Noun Phrase（名詞片語）		present participle（現在分詞）
O	Object（受詞）	sb.	somebody（某人）
OC	Object Complement（受詞補語）	sth.	something（某事）

1

$$S + \begin{cases} \text{look (看起來); sound (聽起來); taste (嚐起來);} \\ \text{smell (聞起來); feel (感覺起來); seem (似乎);} \\ \text{appear (顯得); prove (證明); stay/keep/remain (保持);} \\ \text{turn/become/get/grow (變得)} \end{cases} + \text{adj.}$$

説明▶

1. 本句型中的動詞為連綴動詞用法。連綴動詞在句子中具有連結主詞和主詞補語的作用。連綴動詞後面常接形容詞,用來說明主詞的狀態。

例1 The food tastes delicious.
　　這食物嚐起來很美味。

例2 She always keeps calm.
　　她總是保持冷靜。

例3 Andy's face turned pale when he saw the snake.
　　看到蛇,Andy 的臉變得慘白。

例4 How did the beef noodles taste?
　　牛肉麵嚐起來如何?

2. 某些連綴動詞後面可接 like + N,例如:seem、look、sound、smell、taste、feel 等。

例1 The instant noodles tasted like dirt.
　　這泡麵非常難吃。

例2 The young singer looked like a superstar.
　　這位年輕歌手看起來像一位超級巨星。

例3 What do durians smell like?
　　榴槤聞起來像什麼?

✎ 練功坊

翻譯題

1. 秋天楓葉變紅。

_____

2. 這個模特兒看起來美極了。

_____

3. 這食物嚐起來像牛肉。

_____

4. Alex 看到警察顯得很緊張。

_____

5. 牛奶如果沒放進冰箱，很快就會變酸。

_____

$$S + \begin{cases} \text{see/watch/look at (看到);} \\ \text{hear/listen to (聽);} \\ \text{feel (感覺)/observe (觀察)} \end{cases} + O + OC \text{ (V-ing/V/p.p.)}$$

說明

1. 感官動詞的用法為須在受詞後加受詞補語。
2. 如受詞為主動，則受詞補語為現在分詞 (V-ing) 或原形動詞：現在分詞 (V-ing) 強調動作進行的狀態；原形動詞強調整個動作。

〔例1〕 John heard Mary playing/play the piano in the next room.
John 聽到 Mary 在隔壁房間彈鋼琴。

〔例2〕 Betty saw me riding/ride a bike in the park.
Betty 看到我在公園騎單車。

3. 如受詞為被動，則受詞補語為過去分詞 (p.p.)。

〔例句〕 I saw Fred encouraged by his teacher. 我看到 Fred 被老師鼓勵。

句型比較

$$S + \begin{cases} \text{make/have} + O + OC \text{ (V/p.p.)} \\ \text{let} + O + \begin{cases} OC \text{ (V)} \\ OC \text{ (be + p.p.)} \end{cases} \end{cases} \quad 使\cdots做\cdots$$

說明 1. 使役動詞的用法也是在受詞後加受詞補語。

2. 如受詞為主動，就加原形動詞作為受詞補語；如受詞為被動則加過去分詞 (p.p.)。

3. 注意 let 的被動用法為 let + O + be + p.p.。

例1 My father made me wash the car.
我爸爸叫我洗車。

例2 My mom had my bike fixed yesterday.
我媽媽昨天拿我的腳踏車去修理。

例3 Let the roof be repaired.
讓屋頂被修繕。

延伸補充

help 的用法為 help + O + (to) + V。

例句 Matt helped his mom clean/to clean the house.
Matt 幫他媽媽打掃屋子。

練功坊

翻譯題

1. 我昨天看到 Rick 被很多粉絲包圍。

_____

2. 地震發生時，我感覺到屋子在搖動。

_____

3. 上週我把電腦拿去送修。

_____

3 S + find (發現)/keep (保持)/leave (使得) + O + OC (adj./V-ing/p.p.)

說明

此句型的受詞補語為分詞時，要把握一個原則：主動用現在分詞 (V-ing)，被動則用過去分詞 (p.p.)。也可用形容詞當作受詞補語，用來補充說明受詞的狀態。

例1 The teacher found Jack nodding off in class.

老師發現 Jack 上課打瞌睡。

🖋Tips Jack 打瞌睡，為主動，故受詞補語用現在分詞 nodding。

例2 I found my bike stolen yesterday.

我昨天發現我的腳踏車被偷了。

🖋Tips 腳踏車被偷，為被動，故受詞補語用過去分詞 stolen。

例3 Tom left the back door open.

Tom 讓後門開著。

練功坊

翻譯題

1. 歷史是如此重要，它不應被遺忘。

_____

2. Rick 發現一個小男孩在街上無助地哭泣。

_____

3. 保持環境清潔是每個人的職責。

_____

4

$$S (人) + spend + time/money + \begin{cases} V\text{-ing} \\ on + N \end{cases}$$ 某人花時間或錢做…

$$\begin{cases} S (物) + cost + O (人) + money... \\ It\ cost(s) + O (人) + money + to\ V... \end{cases}$$ 某物花了某人錢…

$$\begin{cases} It\ takes + O (人) + time + to\ V... \\ S (人) + take + time + to\ V... \end{cases}$$ 某人花時間做…

S (人) + take one's time + V-ing 某人不慌不忙做…

[說明]

1. spend 的主詞一定是人；cost 的主詞一定是物或 it。

2. spend 可以指花時間也可以指花錢，表示「某人花時間或錢在…上」；
   cost 指花錢，表示「某物花費某人多少錢」；take 指花時間。

[例1] I spent NT$2,500 buying the new bike/on the new bike.
   → The new bike cost me NT$2,500.
   → It cost me NT$2,500 to buy the new bike.
   這臺新的腳踏車花了我新臺幣 2,500 元。

[例2] It takes me 20 minutes to walk to school every day.
   → I take 20 minutes to walk to school every day.
   → I spend 20 minutes walking to school every day.
   我每天花 20 分鐘走路上學。

3. take one's time + V-ing 有「某人不慌不忙做…」的意思。

[例句] My mother takes her time cooking dinner. 我媽媽不慌不忙地煮晚餐。

練功坊

[翻譯題]

1. Grace 花了四小時跑馬拉松。

_____

2. Jimmy 花了新臺幣 8,000 元買新手機。

_____

5

$$S + \begin{cases} \text{cannot help but + V} \\ \text{cannot help + V-ing} \\ \text{have no choice but + to V} \end{cases} \quad 不得不；忍不住$$

說明▶

此為常用句型，須注意原形動詞、動名詞 (V-ing) 或不定詞的變化。

例1 Since Josh was hungry and thirsty, he could not help but put aside his work and eat.

→ Since Josh was hungry and thirsty, he could not help putting aside his work and eating.

→ Since Josh was hungry and thirsty, he had no choice but to put aside his work and eat.

Josh 因為又渴又餓，不得不把工作放下去吃東西。

例2 Melody could not help but sell her car because she was in need of money.

→ Melody could not help selling her car because she was in need of money.

→ Melody had no choice but to sell her car because she was in need of money.

Melody 因為急需用錢，所以不得不賣掉她的車子。

✎ 練功坊

翻譯題

1. Andy 因為數學不及格，所以不得不上重修課 (make-up class)。

_____

2. 在經濟困難的時期，Allen 不得不省吃儉用。

_____

3. Sandy 一聽到這個笑話就忍不住笑了。

_____

6 S (人) + used to + V　　　　　過去常常做…

$$S (人) + \begin{cases} be \\ get \end{cases} used\ to + \begin{cases} V\text{-ing} \\ N \end{cases} \quad 習慣；適應$$

說明

此句型主詞為人，須注意原形動詞或動名詞 (V-ing) 的變化。

1. 第一個句型表示「過去習慣於…」，此時的 to 為不定詞，所以後面須接原形動詞。

2. 第二個句型表示「現在習慣於…」，此時的 to 為介系詞，所以須接動名詞 (V-ing) 或名詞。而且其中 be 和 get 在語意上略有差異，get 帶有「從原本不習慣轉變為習慣」的含意，be 則並未對這種轉變多作表示。

例1 I used to share my opinions in class.
　　我以前常常在上課時分享意見。

例2 I am used to getting up at six in the morning.
　　我習慣早上六點起床。

例3 I got used to getting up at six in the morning.
　　我習慣了早上六點起床。

句型比較

$$S (物) + be\ used \begin{cases} to + V \\ for + N \end{cases} \quad 被用來…$$

說明 此句型主詞為物，以被動語態表示「某物被用來…」。

例1 The gas stove is used to cook meals.
　　瓦斯爐被用來煮飯。

例2 A lot of herbs are used for flavoring food.
　　很多香草植物都被用來調味食物。

練功坊

翻譯題

1. 我以前一週慢跑三次。

_____

2. 很多外國人不適應臺灣潮溼的天氣。

_____

3. 刀叉被用來切食物。

_____

4. 法律是用來保護人們的權利。

_____

7

$$S + \begin{cases} \text{would rather} + V_1...\text{than} + V_2... \\ \text{prefer} + \underline{V_1\text{-ing/N}}... + \text{to} + \underline{V_2\text{-ing/N}}... \\ \text{prefer to} + V_1...\text{rather than} + V_2... \end{cases} \quad 寧願…而不願…$$

說明▶

本句型須注意動詞 prefer 所搭配的 to 有兩種用法：

1. prefer...to... 的 to 為介系詞，所以須接動名詞 (V-ing) 或名詞。

2. prefer to...rather than... 的 to 則為不定詞，所以須接原形動詞。

例1 David would rather go jogging than stay at home watching TV.

→ David prefers going jogging to staying at home watching TV.

→ David prefers to go jogging rather than stay at home watching TV.

David 寧願去慢跑也不願待在家看電視。

例2 Sarah would rather be single than get married.

→ Sarah prefers being single to getting married.

→ Sarah prefers to be single rather than get married.

Sarah 寧願單身也不願結婚。

練功坊

翻譯題

1. Jimmy 寧願在家吃火鍋也不願去餐廳吃飯。

_____

2. Grace 寧願學習打網球也不願練習瑜珈。

_____

8
$$S + \text{consider} + \text{sb./sth.} + \text{(to be)} + \text{N/adj.}$$
$$S + \begin{Bmatrix} \text{see/view/regard/think of/} \\ \text{look (up)on/take/perceive} \end{Bmatrix} + \text{sb./sth.} + \text{as} + \text{N/adj.} \quad 視\cdots為\cdots$$

S + refer to + sb./sth. + as + N/adj. 　將…稱為…
S + recognize + sb./sth. + as + N/adj. 　認可…

說明▶

本句型須注意上述動詞的用法，主要是在受詞後，以 as 接名詞或形容詞當受詞補語；只有 consider 是以 to be 接名詞或形容詞當受詞補語，並且 to be 可以省略。

例1 George Washington is seen/viewed as one of the Founding Fathers of the U.S.

→ George Washington is regarded/taken/perceived as one of the Founding Fathers of the U.S.

→ George Washington is thought of/looked (up)on as one of the Founding Fathers of the U.S.

華盛頓被認為是美國的開國元勳之一。

例2 The drunk driver was seen/viewed as guilty.

→ The drunk driver was regarded/taken/perceived as guilty.

→ The drunk driver was thought of/looked (up)on as guilty.

這名酒醉的駕駛被認為有罪。

✎ 練功坊

翻譯題

1. 父母通常認為玩線上遊戲是在浪費時間。

_____

2. 這門學科被認為非常重要。

_____

9

S (人) +
$\begin{cases} \text{inform (通知); remind (使想起);} \\ \text{convince (使…信服); rob (搶);} \\ \text{deprive (剝奪); accuse (控告);} \\ \text{relieve (減輕); cure (治癒)} \end{cases}$ + sb. + of + N...

說明

此句型的動詞通常先接人(間接受詞),然後再以 of 接事物(直接受詞)。注意此句型不論是主動式還是被動式,of 皆不能省略。

例1 We informed Jack of the good news.
　　我們通知 Jack 這個好消息。

例2 The police tried to convince Tom of the fact that his son was a thief.
　　警方試著使 Tom 相信他兒子是個小偷。

例3 The doctor successfully cured Tim of the serious disease.
　　醫生成功地治癒 Tim 嚴重的疾病。

例4 No one should be deprived of the freedom of speech.
　　任何人都不應被剝奪言論自由。

✎ 練功坊

翻譯題

1. Dave 被控謀殺。

_____

2. 這個男人搶了 Betty 昂貴的包包。

_____

3. 這張照片讓 Rick 想起他摯愛的奶奶。

_____

10

$$A + \begin{cases} \text{comprise} \\ \text{consist of} \\ \text{be \underline{comprised}/\underline{composed} of} \\ \text{be made up of} \end{cases} + B \quad \text{A 是由 B 所組成的}$$

說明

本句型表示「…由…組成」之意，在此句型中，consist of 不能使用被動式；comprise 則是使用主動式或被動式皆可，並且和 compose 及 make up 一樣，在被動句中須加 of。

例句 The class comprises 14 boy students and 20 girl students.

→ The class consists of 14 boy students and 20 girl students.

→ The class is comprised/composed of 14 boy students and 20 girl students.

→ The class is made up of 14 boy students and 20 girl students.

這班級是由 14 個男學生和 20 個女學生所組成的。

練功坊

翻譯題

1. 這個組織是由美國、加拿大及 27 個歐洲國家所組成的。

_____

2. 全體員工是由義大利人與美國人所組成的。

_____

11 $S + \begin{cases} \text{be + located/situated...} \\ \text{stand/sit/lie...} \end{cases}$ …位於…

說明

在此句型中，located 和 situated 用被動，而 stand、sit 和 lie 則須用主動。兩者都常以分詞構句的形式出現，也都常出現於大考的綜合測驗題型。

例1 Located/Situated on the main road, Dr. Sun Yat-sen Memorial Hall was built in memory of Dr. Sun Yat-sen.

國父紀念館位於主要幹道上，是建來紀念孫中山先生的。

Tips 此為 Dr. Sun Yat-sen Memorial Hall is located/situated on the main road. 與 Dr. Sun Yat-sen Memorial Hall was built in memory of Dr. Sun Yat-sen. 兩句合併改寫而成。因 be located/situated 為被動形式，故合併後開頭用過去分詞 (p.p.)。

例2 Standing/Sitting/Lying on the main road, Dr. Sun Yat-sen Memorial Hall was built in memory of Dr. Sun Yat-sen.

國父紀念館位於主要幹道上，是建來紀念孫中山先生的。

Tips 此為 Dr. Sun Yat-sen Memorial Hall stands/sits/lies on the main road. 與 Dr. Sun Yat-sen Memorial Hall was built in memory of Dr. Sun Yat-sen. 兩句合併改寫而成。因 stand/sit/lie 為主動形式，故合併後開頭用現在分詞 (V-ing)。

例3 The coffee shop is located/situated on the street corner; you can easily find it.

→ The coffee shop stands/sits/lies on the street corner; you can easily find it.

這家咖啡廳位於街角，你可以很容易找到它。

練功坊

翻譯題

1. 這間博物館位於嘉義 (Chiayi)。

_____

2. 墾丁國家公園位於臺灣南部。

_____

3. 我家在東臺灣的一個小漁村。

_____

12 S + happen (+ to sb.)...　…發生 (在某人身上)

　　S + occur...　(天災等) 發生

說明▶

這兩個句型都不能用被動式。其中 occur 常用來指意外或災害發生。

例1 Something funny happened to Andy last night. He was mistaken for a singer.
昨晚有件趣事發生在 Andy 身上。他被誤認為是一位歌手。

例2 An earthquake occurred in China last week and killed many people.
上週中國發生地震，很多人喪生。

句型比較▶

★ S + happen to V...　…碰巧…

★ S + belong to...　…屬於…

★ S + take place...　…舉行…

★ It occurs to sb. that + 子句　…突然想到…

說明 以上這些句型也都不能用被動式。

例1 Daniel happened to meet his high school classmate on the street yesterday.
Daniel 昨天在街上碰巧遇到他的高中同學。

例2 The ring belongs to the young lady standing there.
這只戒指屬於站在那裡的那位年輕小姐。

例3 The athletic meet takes place in June every year.
運動會每年六月舉行。

例4 On my way home yesterday, it occurred to me that I left my wallet on the office desk.
昨天回家途中，我突然想到我把皮夾留在辦公桌上了。

✏ 練功坊

翻譯題

1. 昨天有幸運的事發生在 Alex 身上，所以他很高興。

_____

2. 發生一場龍捲風，毀了小鎮上 40 棟房子。

_____

3. 這個袋子屬於這位留長髮的小女孩。

_____

4. 我們校慶每年十一月舉行。

_____

Chapter 2　助動詞相關句型

13

$$S + have/has + p.p. \begin{cases} + \text{for} + \text{一段時間} \\ + \text{since} + \text{過去式子句 (+ 一段時間 + ago)} \\ + \text{since} + \text{年代／季節／月分} \\ + \text{so far (目前為止)} \\ + \text{over the past years (過去幾年)/} \\ \quad \text{in recent years (近幾年)} \\ + \text{for a long time/for ages (很久了)} \end{cases}$$

說明▶

此為現在完成式的句子，在大考常出現。此句型須特別注意時間副詞的變化，通常用時間副詞來判斷是否要用現在完成式，常用於在本句型中表示時間的字詞有 in recent years、for a long time、since 等。

例1 I have lived in Taipei for 20 years.

　　我在臺北已經住 20 年了。

例2 She has lived in the UK since she got married ten years ago.

　　她十年前結婚時就已經住在英國了。

例3 I have known Bill since he was a college student.

　　Bill 還是大學生的時候我就認識他了。

例4 Stone tools have been used as weapons and cutting tools for ages.

　　石器被用來當武器和切割工具已經很久了。

練功坊

翻譯題

1. Tom 從去年夏天就一直待在日本。

_____

2. 近幾年來手機被廣泛使用。

_____

3. Helen 目前為止尚未去過美國。

_____

14 By the time + S + V-ed..., S + had + p.p. ⋯的時候，⋯已經⋯
By the time + S + V..., S will have + p.p. ⋯的時候，⋯將已經⋯

_____

說明

此句型須注意有兩種時態，一種用來陳述過去已經發生的事，另一種用來陳述未來將會發生的事。本句型前後的主詞可以不同。

例1 By the time Andy reached the train station, the train had left.

Andy 到達火車站時，火車已經離開了。

Tips 陳述過去已經發生的事。

例2 By the time Bob reaches the train station, the train will have left.

Bob 到達火車站時，火車將會已經離開。

Tips 陳述未來將會發生的事。

例3 By the time Daniel saw a doctor, he had been sick for two weeks.

Daniel 去看醫生時已經生病兩週了。

例4 By the time Jeff finishes building the house, he will have built five houses.

Jeff 蓋完這棟房子時，他將已經蓋好五棟房子了。

練功坊

翻譯題

1. David 完成這本書時，他將已經寫了三本了。

_____

2. Steve 與 Nancy 結婚時，他們已經交往十年了。

_____

3. 九月學校開學時，我就會成為高三生了。

_____

15 $S + \begin{cases} \text{must} + V \\ \text{must} + \text{have} + \text{p.p.} \end{cases}$ 一定…

說明

1. must + V 表示對現在很有把握的猜測。

2. must + have + p.p. 表示對過去很有把握的猜測。

例1 Tom is going to give a speech in five minutes. He must be very nervous.

　　Tom 五分鐘後要演講，他一定很緊張。

例2 I must have seen the movie before.

　　我以前一定看過這部電影。

句型比較

★ S + should have + p.p.　應該…才對

★ S + might/may/could have + p.p.　也許…；可能…

說明 1. should have + p.p. 表示過去該做而沒做的事。

　　　2. might/may/could have + p.p. 帶有假設語氣的意味，表示本來可以做或是可能發生的事。

例1 May failed her math test last semester. She should have studied harder.

　　上學期 May 數學考試不及格，她應該更用功一點。(表示應該要用功而沒用功)

例2 Sandra might have married her boss.

　　Sandra 本來可能嫁給她老闆。(結果沒有嫁)

例3 She could have helped me with my homework.

　　她本來可以協助我做作業的。(結果沒有協助我)

練功坊

翻譯題

1. 我的皮夾一定是放在抽屜裡。

2. Peter 昨晚一定是喝醉了。

_____

3. 我上星期應繳交報告才對。

_____

4. 他們可能已成立了新公司。

_____

16

$$S + \begin{cases} \text{suggest (建議); recommend (推薦);} \\ \text{advise (勸告); insist (堅持);} \\ \text{request (請求); demand, require (要求);} \\ \text{command, order (命令)} \end{cases} + \text{that} + S \ (+ \text{should}) + V$$

說明▶

上列這些動詞以 that 接子句，子句都用原形動詞，這是因為省略了 should。

例如這兩個英文句子：My father suggested something. 與 He asked me to go to bed early.

可以合併成一句：My father suggested that I (should) go to bed early. 爸爸提議我早點睡。

例1 Our teacher insisted that we turn in/hand in/submit our homework/ assignments on time.

老師堅持我們要準時交作業。

例2 My homeroom teacher recommended that Fred participate in/take part in the English speech contest.

班導推薦 Fred 參加英文演講比賽。

練功坊

翻譯題

1. 皇帝下令 Valentine 要被處死。

_____

2. 爸爸勸告我晚上 11 點前回家。

_____

3. 這家公司要求每個員工穿制服。

_____

17

$$S + V_1... + \begin{cases} \text{for fear of + N/V}_2\text{-ing...} \\ \text{for fear that + S + would/will/might/may + V}_2... \\ \text{lest + S (+ should) + V}_2... \end{cases} \text{以免}$$

說明

此句型須注意，lest 後所接子句中的 should 通常都省略，所以須接原形動詞。

例1 I studied hard for fear of failing the exam.

→ I studied hard for fear that I might fail the exam.

→ I studied hard lest I (should) fail the exam.

我努力讀書以免考試不及格。

例2 She always locks the two locks in the door for fear of being robbed.

→ She always locks the two locks in the door for fear that she might be robbed.

→ She always locks the two locks in the door lest she (should) be robbed.

她總是把門鎖兩道以免被搶。

練功坊

翻譯題

1. Daniel 今天早上提早出門，以免交通阻塞。

_____

2. Grace 跟 Tim 說了一個善意的謊言，以免傷害他的感情。

_____

18
$$\begin{cases} \text{To/In order to} + V_1..., \ S + V_2... \\ S + V_2... + \text{to/in order to} + V_1... \end{cases} \quad 為了\cdots$$

說明

To/In order to 為表目的之用法，除放置句首外，也可以改成小寫放置在句中。

例句 To/In order to score well on the college entrance exam and go to a good college, Tom studies hard.

→ Tom studies hard to/in order to score well on the college entrance exam and go to a good college.

Tom 用功讀書是為了在大學入學考試中得到好成績，進入一所好大學。

句型替換

$$S + V_1... + \begin{bmatrix} \text{so as to} \\ \text{with a view to/with an eye to} \\ \text{in order that/so that} \end{bmatrix} + \begin{bmatrix} V_2 \\ V_2\text{-ing/N} \\ 子句 \end{bmatrix}$$

說明 1. 此組句型也是表目的，其中的 so as to 不可放置於句首；而 in order that 接子句為較正式的用法。

2. 此組句型的動詞變化也須留意：so as to 須接原形動詞，因為此處 to 為不定詞的用法。with a view to/with an eye to 則須接動名詞 (V-ing) 或名詞，因為此處 to 為介系詞的用法。

例句 Tom studies hard so as to score well on the college entrance exam and go to a good college.

→ Tom studies hard with a view to/with an eye to scoring well on the college entrance exam and going to a good college.

→ Tom studies so hard in order that/so that he can score well on the college entrance exam and go to a good college.

Tom 用功讀書是為了在大學入學考試中得到好成績，進入一所好大學。

✏️練功坊

翻譯題

1. 為了工作有效率，你需要良好的時間管理。

_____

2. 為了慶祝新年，美國家庭十二月底相聚在一起。

_____

 19 To V_1/V_1-ing... + V_2...

說明

此句型為不定詞或動名詞 (V-ing) 當主詞的用法，這樣的主詞之後須接單數動詞。

例1 To get to school on time is necessary for students.

→ Getting to school on time is necessary for students.

對學生來說，準時到校是必需的。

🔦Tips 本例第一句的主詞為不定詞片語 To get to school on time，動詞為 is。第二句的主詞為動名詞片語 Getting to school on time，動詞為 is。

例2 To conserve endangered species is important.

→ Conserving endangered species is important.

保護瀕臨滅絕的物種很重要。

🔦Tips 本例第一句的主詞為不定詞片語 To conserve endangered species，動詞為 is。第二句的主詞為動名詞片語 Conserving endangered species，動詞為 is。

句型比較

★ 分詞構句：V_1-ing..., S + V_2...

★ 祈使句：V_1..., and/or S + V_2...

★ 不定詞：To V_1..., S + V_2...

說明 分詞構句、祈使句和不定詞表目的的句型，以及不定詞或動名詞 (V-ing) 當主詞的用法，常在大考的選擇題中同時出現作為誘答選項，須注意其差異與變化。

1. 分詞構句，將連接詞與對應的主詞去掉，並將對應的動詞改成現在分詞 (V-ing)，就可以成為分詞構句。

例1 Getting up at 6 a.m. every morning, Ted gets to school on time.

Ted 因為每天早上六點起床所以都準時到校。

> Tips 此例句為典型的分詞構句，可還原為 Because Ted gets up at 6 a.m. every morning, he gets to school on time. 這樣的原句。將前半段的連接詞 because 與主詞 Ted 去掉，並將動詞 gets 改成 getting，就可以改為分詞構句。

例2 Answering his teacher's questions correctly, Tim got a prize.

Tim 因為正確回答老師的問題而獲得獎賞。

> Tips 本例的原句為 Because Tim answered his teacher's questions correctly, he got a prize.。

2. 祈使句為省略主詞 you，直接以原形動詞為起首句子。

例1 Get to school on time, or you will get punished.

準時到校，否則你會被處罰。

> Tips 本句為將 (You) Get to school on time, or you will get punished. 中原本在句首的 You 省略，改以原形動詞 Get 起首的祈使句。

例2 (You) Stand up and answer the question, please.

請站起來回答這個問題。

3. 不定詞可放在句首表目的。

例1 To get to school on time, Tom gets up at 6 a.m. every morning.

→ In order to get to school on time, Tom gets up at 6 a.m. every morning.

為了準時到校，Tom 每天早上六點起床。

> Tips 本句以不定詞表目的，To 可以替換成 In order to。

例2 In order to achieve his goals, Rick works hard day and night.

為了達成目標，Rick 日夜努力工作。

例3 To get to the destination earlier, Tina hits the road soon.

為了提早到達目的地，Tina 很快就上路了。

✎ 練功坊

選擇題

( ) 1. ____ people in need, Jimmy feels happy.

    (A) To help   (B) Help   (C) Helping   (D) Helped

( ) 2. ____ people in need, Jimmy decides to work as a volunteer.

    (A) To help   (B) Help   (C) Helping   (D) Helped

( ) 3. ____ others makes you happy.

    (A) In order to help   (B) Help

    (C) Helping   (D) Helped

( ) 4. ____ people in need, and you will feel happy every day.

    (A) To help   (B) Help   (C) Helping   (D) Helped

20

S + have + $\begin{cases} \text{trouble/difficulty/} \\ \text{a hard time/problems} \end{cases}$ + (in) V-ing　很難做…

說明 ▶

1. 此句型要搭配動名詞 (V-ing)，因為其中常被省略的 in 是介系詞。

2. 此句型可用 It is difficult + for sb. + to V 改寫。

例1 The depressed father had trouble getting along with his family.

  → It was difficult for the depressed father to get along with his family.

  這位意志消沉的父親很難跟家人和睦相處。

例2 The students had problems solving these math questions.

  → It was difficult for the students to solve these math questions.

  這些學生難以解出這些數學問題。

例3 The old man had difficulty swallowing.

  → It was difficult for the old man to swallow.

  這個老人吞嚥有困難。

延伸用法

S + ┌ consider (考慮); contemplate (沉思);
    │ suggest (建議); mind (介意); finish (完成);   + V-ing
    └ practice (練習); enjoy (享受); imagine (想像)

說明 以上列出的這些動詞都在其後直接加 V-ing，不加 to。

例句 I consider going to the movies with my mom tonight.
     我考慮今晚跟我媽媽去看電影。

練功坊

翻譯題

1. 沒有別人的幫忙，人們難以過得好。

_____

2. 一般人沒有適當的訓練很難跑馬拉松。

_____

3. 你能想像住在外太空的生活嗎？

_____

21 There is no + V-ing...　無法…；不可能…；沒有…

說明

此句型的 V-ing 為動名詞，接在慣用語 There is no 之後，表示「難以…」。

例1 There is no telling/knowing if the result will satisfy us.
     無法得知結果會不會讓我們滿意。

例2 There is no accounting for taste.
     人的喜好是無法解釋的。

句型比較

There + be + N + V-ing/p.p.　有…正在…；有…被…

說明 此句型以分詞當補語，主動用現在分詞 (V-ing)，被動用過去分詞 (p.p.)。

例1 There are some students playing word games.

有些學生在玩填字遊戲。

　　Tips 本句原為 There are some students who are playing word games.，可將關係子句中的 who are 省略，以分詞改寫。學生玩填字遊戲為主動，故用現在分詞 playing。

例2 There are no used books sold in the bookstore.

這家書店沒賣二手書。

　　Tips 本句原為 There are no used books which are sold in the bookstore.，可將關係子句中的 which are 省略，以分詞改寫。二手書被販賣，故用過去分詞 sold。

例3 There is one couple swimming in the pool.

有一對情侶在游泳池裡游泳。

例4 There are some delicious desserts made in Taiwan.

有些美味的甜點是在臺灣做的。

練功坊

翻譯題

1. 無法預測颱風什麼時候會侵襲這個小島。

_____

2. 此區禁止停車。

_____

3. 有些人抗議居住不正義 (injustice of housing)。

_____

4. 在偏遠的村莊有些小孩無法上學。

_____

22 V₁-ing/p.p...., S + V₂...　(分詞構句)

說明

此句型為典型的分詞構句，是在前後主詞相同時，將連接詞與附屬子句主詞

省略後改寫而成的句型。句意如果為主動，須將附屬子句的動詞改為現在分詞 (V-ing)，如為被動則改為過去分詞 (p.p.)。

例1 As Joe did not know what to do, he just stood there.

→ Not knowing what to do, Joe just stood there.

Joe 不知該怎麼辦，只是站在那裡。

Tips as 為連接詞，前後兩部分的主詞指的都是 Joe，故可改成分詞構句。因句意為主動、否定，改寫時須以現在分詞 (V-ing) 搭配否定詞 not，故用 not knowing。

例2 The boy was punished by his father. The boy began to cry.

→ Punished by his father, the boy began to cry.

這男孩被他爸爸處罰，開始哭了起來。

Tips 前後兩句的主詞指的都是 the boy，故可改成分詞構句。因句意為被動，合併須以過去分詞 (p.p.) 改寫，故用 punished。

例3 Praised by his mom, Joseph had a good mood all day.

Joseph 受到他媽媽的稱讚，整天都有好心情。

例4 Having confidence and determination, Jane did everything well.

Jane 有信心和決心，每件事都做得很好。

句型比較

$S_1 + V_1$-ing/p.p...., $S_2 + V_2$...　　(獨立分詞構句)

說明 此句型為獨立分詞構句，用在前後主詞不同時。此句型也是根據句意，主動用現在分詞 (V-ing)，被動則用過去分詞 (p.p.)。須注意前後兩個不同的主詞都必須寫出來，都不能省略。

例1 Because it was a sunny day, we decided to go for a picnic.

→ It being a sunny day, we decided to go for a picnic.

天氣晴朗，我們決定去野餐。

Tips 改寫時，連接詞 because 可省略，was 改成 being。但是因為前後兩部分的主詞不同，前為 it，後為 we，故主詞不能省略。(只有當前後主詞一致時，前主詞才可省略。)

例2 Daniel feeling ill today, we cancelled the meeting.

因為 Daniel 今天感覺身體不適，我們取消會議。

練功坊

[翻譯題]

1. 那些海鮮是從超市買來的，非常新鮮。

_____

2. 小偷發現四周無人就闖入屋內了。

_____

23

$$\begin{cases} \text{With + NP, S + V...} \\ \text{S + V...(,) with + O + OC} \end{cases}$$ （表狀態）

說明

名詞片語為一組字群當名詞用；受詞補語可為形容詞或分詞片語，主動時用現在分詞 (V-ing)，被動用過去分詞 (p.p.)。

[例1] If you make a little more efforts, you will surely succeed.

→ With a little more efforts, you will surely succeed.

多一點努力，你一定會成功。

[例2] With imagination and a good command of language, you might be able to create an interesting novel.

擁有想像力和良好的語言掌握能力，你也許能寫出有趣的小說。

[例3] Susan is riding her bike with her hair blowing in the wind.

Susan 騎著單車，頭髮隨風飛揚。

[例4] My grandfather was sitting on the sofa listening to the radio, with his eyes closed.

我爺爺閉著眼睛，坐在沙發上聽收音機。

[例5] The beggar was lying on the street, with some coins in his hand.

乞丐躺在街上，手裡還有些硬幣。

練功坊

翻譯題

1. 我爸爸坐在椅子上，翹著二郎腿。

_____

2. Mary 不回答，一直搖頭。

_____

3. 老婦人一言不發，淚流滿面。

_____

24

$$S + V, \begin{cases} \text{including...} \\ \text{...included} \\ \text{inclusive of...} \end{cases} \quad \cdots 包括\cdots$$

說明

1. 此句型的逗點左邊皆為一個完整的句子。逗點右邊若為形容詞片語 inclusive of，將受詞放在介系詞 of 之後即可。

2. 逗點右邊若用分詞片語，須注意受詞放在後面時，就要先寫現在分詞 including；受詞放在前面時，則須接過去分詞 included。

例1 Ten mountaineers got lost in the mountains, including Jeff and his girlfriend.

→ Ten mountaineers got lost in the mountains, Jeff and his girlfriend included.

→ Ten mountaineers got lost in the mountains, inclusive of Jeff and his girlfriend.

十個登山客在山中迷路，包括 Jeff 和他女友。

例2 50 students competed in the speech contest, including George and Mary.

→ 50 students competed in the speech contest, George and Mary included.

→ 50 students competed in the speech contest, inclusive of George and Mary.

50 個學生參加演講比賽，包括 George 和 Mary。

練功坊

翻譯題

1. 30 個人在車禍中喪生，包括駕駛和導遊。

_____

2. 七個人中樂透，包括 David 和他兒子。

_____

25

one...the other...	(兩者中的) 一個…另一個…
one...another...the other...	(三者中的) 一個…一個…另一個…
one...another...	(未指明多少) 一個…另一個…
one...another...still another...	(未指明多少) 一個…一個…另一個…
some of...the others...	(有限定範圍) 一些…其餘…
some...others...	(沒有限定範圍) 一些…一些…
some...others...still others...	(沒有限定範圍) 一些…一些…還有一些…

說明

此句型須注意「有限定範圍」和「沒有限定範圍」的用法差異，有限定範圍時須搭配使用定冠詞 the。 其中 one...another...still another... 以及 some...others...still others... 尤其為大考常見句型。

例1 Some of the students in the class studied hard; the others didn't.
這個班級裡有一些學生很努力，其餘則不然。

　Tips 有限定在 in the class 的範圍當中， 所以須搭配使用定冠詞 the， 故使用 Some of...the others...。

例2 Some students studied hard; others didn't.
有些學生很努力，有些沒有。

　Tips 泛指一般學生，沒有限定範圍，故使用 Some...others...。

例3 I have two sisters. One is a nurse, and the other is a teacher.
我有兩個姊姊。一個是護士，另一個是老師。

例4 I have three sisters. One is a nurse, another is a teacher, and the other is a factory worker.
我有三個姊姊。一個是護士，一個是老師，另一個是工廠工人。

例5 I don't like this one. Please give me another.
我不喜歡這個，請給我另一個。

例6 Here, there is one restroom for women, another for men, and still another for the disabled.

這裡有一個女用廁所，一個男用廁所，還有一個無障礙廁所。

〔例7〕 Some birds are black, others are white, and still others are red.

有些鳥是黑的，有些是白的，還有些是紅的。

練功坊

選擇題

(   ) 1. One of my parents is an office worker; ____ is a bus driver.

      (A) another   (B) other   (C) the other   (D) still the other

(   ) 2. I don't like this watermelon. Please give me ____.

      (A) another   (B) other   (C) the other   (D) still the other

(   ) 3. One of the three students is from Africa, another is from Japan and ____ is from Taiwan.

      (A) still another   (B) the other   (C) other   (D) the others

(   ) 4. Some of the students from America like Taiwanese food; ____ don't.

      (A) the others   (B) another   (C) others   (D) still others

(   ) 5. Some students enjoy jogging, others enjoy playing tennis and ____ enjoy playing music.

      (A) the others   (B) others   (C) still others   (D) the other

---

26 someone, somebody; something; anyone; anything; nobody; nothing + adj.

說明

形容詞通常置於名詞前面。但以上這幾個代名詞被形容詞修飾時，形容詞須置於這些字後面。

〔例1〕 He doesn't want to make friends with someone arrogant.

他不想跟傲慢的人交朋友。

〔例2〕 Tell me something interesting.

跟我講點有趣的事。

例3 Is anyone absent from today's meeting?

今天的會議有人缺席嗎？

例4 Did anything important happen last week?

上週有任何重要的事發生嗎？

例5 There's nothing new under the sun.

太陽底下沒有新鮮事。

練功坊

翻譯題

1. 下週三有特別的人要來參訪我們學校。

_____

2. 我真的不想說有關於他的任何壞事。

_____

3. 昨天沒什麼糟糕的事發生。

_____

27

S + have +
- a lot/much　　　　　　　與…有很大的關係
- something　　　　　　　與…有關係
- a little　　+ to do with...　與…有一點關係
- little　　　　　　　　　　與…沒什麼關係
- nothing　　　　　　　　　與…沒有關係

說明

此句型用來表示「關聯性」，各組用語的用法相同，只有程度上的差異，可以當作片語來背。

例1 The murder case has nothing to do with the official.

這起謀殺案與這位官員無關。

例2 The failure of the project has something to do with the budget.

案子的失敗與預算有關。

例3 Tom's success has a lot to do with diligence.

Tom 的成功和勤勞很有關係。

例4 Daniel's winning the lottery has a little to do with luck.

Daniel 中樂透與運氣有點關係。

✎練功坊

翻譯題

1. 火災跟 Rick 的疏失有很大的關係。

_____

2. 這個城市的繁榮和它的市長有些關係。

_____

3. Alex 優秀的表現與他的個性有點關係。

_____

Chapter 5　　形容詞與副詞相關句型

28　be + adj. = be + of + N

說明▶

此句型是將形容詞以 of + N 的方式改寫。名詞前面也可加上 such、great 等字作為修飾。

例1 Time management is important to everyone.

→ Time management is of importance to everyone.

時間管理對每個人都很重要。

例2 The vase was so valuable that Kevin put it in the safe at home.

→ The vase was of such value that Kevin put it in the safe at home.

這花瓶是如此寶貴，所以 Kevin 把它放在家裡的保險箱。

例3 The old clock is significant to the Lin family.

→ The old clock is of great significance to the Lin family.

這老舊的時鐘對林家人意義重大。

練功坊

翻譯題

1. 開車時遵守交通規則很重要。

_____

2. 我真的沒有任何值錢的東西。

_____

29　{ (Much) to the N of sb., S + V...
　　　　{ (Much) to one's N, S + V...　令⋯(高興／難過) 的是⋯

說明

此句型中的 much 可省略；逗點後直接加句子，不須加連接詞。

例1 (Much) to the delight of my parents, my brother won first prize in the contest.

→ (Much) to my parents' delight, my brother won first prize in the contest.

令我父母很高興的是，我哥哥比賽得第一名。

例2 (Much) to the satisfaction of Steve, his son cooks better than he does.

→ (Much) to Steve's satisfaction, his son cooks better than he does.

令 Steve 很滿意的是，他兒子比他會做菜。

例3 (Much) to the surprise of me, Frank hit the jackpot.

→ (Much) to my surprise, Frank hit the jackpot.

讓我很驚訝的是，Frank 中了頭彩。

例4 (Much) to the shock of Andy, his girlfriend married another man.

→ (Much) to Andy's shock, his girlfriend married another man.

令 Andy 震驚的是，他女友跟別人結婚了。

例5 (Much) to the dismay of my uncle, his wife died of cancer last week.

→ (Much) to my uncle's dismay, his wife died of cancer last week.

令我舅舅很難過的是，他太太上週死於癌症。

練功坊

翻譯題

1. 讓他很後悔的是，他沒去參加他女兒的畢業典禮。

_____

2. 我很驚訝，上週他跟 Tina 分手了。

_____

3. 讓 Darren 和他弟弟很高興的是，他爸爸買了一間新房子。

_____

4. 讓她很高興的是，同學會出乎意料地成功。

_____

30

$$\begin{cases} \text{a lot/much/far} \\ \text{slightly/a little/a bit} \\ \text{even/still} \end{cases} + \text{比較級}$$

比…得多
比…一點
比…還更…

說明▶

比較級的前面，原則上不加 the，但可加上面所列的修飾詞。

例1 The river is a lot/much/far cleaner than before.

河流比以前乾淨得多。

例2 Brisk walking is slightly/a little/a bit easier than running.

快走比跑步簡單一點。

例3 Book One is even/still harder than Book Two.

第一冊甚至比第二冊還更難。

句型比較▶

★ the very/much the + 最高級　最…

★ very + 原級　很…，非常…

說明 1. 最高級的前面可加 the very 或 much the 當作修飾詞。

2. 原級的前面則是可加 very 當作修飾詞。

例1 Allen is the very most handsome boy in his class.

Allen 是他班上最英俊的男生。

例2 Taipei 101 was once much the tallest building in the world.

臺北 101 一度是世界上最高的大樓。

例3 We're very sorry to see you go.

看到你要離開了，我們都很難過。

✎練功坊

翻譯題

1. 玉山比阿里山高很多。

2. 搭捷運比騎公共自行車貴一點。

_____

3. 在臺灣騎機車比在美國還要更普遍。

_____

4. Linda 非常感謝她父母的幫助。

_____

 31
$$\begin{cases} \text{The more} + S + V_1..., \text{the more} + S + V_2... \\ \text{The} + 比較級 + S + V_1..., \text{the} + 比較級 + S + V_2... \end{cases}$$ 越…越…

說明

比較級通常不加 the，但此特殊句型表示「越…越…」，一定要用 the 加上比較級。

例1 The more I get to know the students here, the better/more I like them.
　　我越了解這裡的學生，就越喜歡他們。

例2 The more you eat, the heavier you get.
　　你吃得越多就越胖。

例3 The older people get, the wiser they are.
　　人年紀越大，越有智慧。

練功坊

翻譯題

1. 你越運動就越健康。

_____

2. 我吃得越健康越覺得舒暢。

_____

3. 你越快樂，就越長壽。

_____

4. 你想要的越少，你就越滿足。

32

$$S_1 + V_1 + 倍數 + \begin{cases} as + adj./adv. + as + S_2 (+ V_2) \\ 比較級 + than + S_2 (+ V_2) \\ the\ N\ of + S_2 \end{cases}$$

說明

此組句型原則上先寫倍數。注意第一個句型 as...as 中間須用形容詞或副詞的原級；第二個句型則須用比較級加 than。

例1 This bridge is three times as long as that one.
→ This bridge is three times longer than that one.
→ This bridge is three times the length of that one.
這座橋是那座橋的三倍長。

例2 Tom's shirt is twice as large as David's.
→ Tom's shirt is two times larger than David's.
→ Tom's shirt is twice the size of David's.
Tom 的襯衫是 David 的兩倍大。

例3 I earn three times as much as Fred (does).
→ I earn three times more than Fred (does).
我賺的是 Fred 的三倍。

練功坊

翻譯題

1. 這棟建築是那棟的六倍高。

2. 這部跑車是那部的四倍貴。

3. 我的土地是你的五倍大。

_____

33

$$S_1 + V_1 + \begin{cases} \text{as/so + adj./adv. + as} \\ \text{as many + N + as} \\ \text{as much + N + as} \end{cases} + S_2 (+ V_2) \quad 跟…一樣…$$

_____

說明▶

1. 此句型中的形容詞或副詞都用原級。

例句 He is as tall as Tim.

　　他跟 Tim 一樣高。

2. 此句型的否定用 not so...as... 或 not as...as...。

例句 Betty did not run so/as fast as Grace (did).

　　Betty 跑得不像 Grace 一樣快。

3. 此句型須注意複數名詞要搭配使用 many；不可數名詞則搭配使用 much。

例1 Rick has as many books as I (do).

　　Rick 有跟我一樣多的書。

例2 The house has as much space as that one (does).

　　這房子有跟那棟一樣多的空間。

✎練功坊

翻譯題

1. 她跟她姊姊一樣努力工作。

_____

2. 超市不像夜市一樣吵雜。

_____

3. Fred 喝的水和 Alex 一樣多。

_____

34

$$S + V + as + adj./adv. + as + \begin{cases} possible \\ sb.\ can \end{cases}$$ 盡可能⋯，盡量⋯

說明

此句型中的形容詞或副詞都用原級。此句型的後半段可用 as possible，也可用搭配主詞的代名詞，改寫成 as sb. can 的形式。

例1 I will hand in the paper as soon as possible.

→ I will hand in the paper as soon as I can.

我會盡快交報告。

例2 Steve ran as fast as possible.

→ Steve ran as fast as he could.

Steve 盡可能跑快一些。

例3 David tried to finish the project as well as possible.

→ David tried to finish the project as well as he could.

David 盡量試著把企劃好好完成。

練功坊

翻譯題

1. Jane 承諾盡快還書。

_____

2. Brad 試著盡可能仔細聽。

_____

3. 我會盡量把工作做好。

_____

Chapter 6　介系詞相關句型

35		
look forward to		期盼…
be/get used to		習慣…；適應…
<u>devote sth./yourself to</u>	+ N/V-ing	把…用於／致力於…
What do you say to		覺得…如何
<u>be opposed to</u>/<u>object to</u>		反對…

說明

此句型常在大考出現，其中的 to 為介系詞，後須接名詞或動名詞 (V-ing)。

例1 I am looking forward to seeing my family soon.
我期待很快看到我的家人。

例2 We are used to the buzzing noise from the engine.
我們習慣了從這引擎發出的嗡嗡的噪音。

例3 Mother Teresa devoted her life to helping poor people.
德蕾莎修女一生致力於幫助窮人。

✎ 練功坊

翻譯題

1. Tom 反對做父母叫他做的事。

_____

2. 他很期待跟他的好友再相見。

_____

3. 他致力於改善他社區的生活品質。

_____

36 prevent/stop/keep/ prohibit/bar/deter + N + from + N/V-ing 阻止，使得…無法…

說明

此句型在介系詞 from 後加名詞或動名詞 (V-ing)，表示「阻止，使得…無法…」。

例1 Does the death penalty prohibit the crimes from happening again?
死刑是否阻止犯罪再次發生？

例2 Keeping early hours prevents Jason from being late for work.
早睡早起使得 Jason 上班不會遲到。

例3 Washing hands frequently can keep you from getting infections.
常洗手可避免你得到傳染病。

句型比較

protect...from + N/V-ing 保護…免於…

說明 此句型中也是在介系詞 from 後加名詞或動名詞 (V-ing)，但注意此句型的意思為「保護…免於…」。

例1 Wearing a life vest can protect you from drowning.
穿救生衣可保護你避免溺水。

例2 The coat can protect your children from colds.
這件大衣可以保護你的小孩免於著涼。

練功坊

翻譯題

1. 運動前熱身可以避免你受傷。

_____

2. 壞天氣使得我們無法去花蓮旅遊。

_____

3. 一場突如其來的車禍使得這對夫婦無法準時到達婚宴。

_____

37 be + $\begin{cases} \text{famous/noted/known/} \\ \text{well-known/renowned} \end{cases}$ + for/as...　以⋯聞名

說明

此句型須判斷 for 和 as 的用法：

1. for + 動作、行為、事蹟、特色。

2. as + 身分、職業、別稱。

例1 Hsinchu is famous for its meatballs.

新竹以貢丸聞名。

Tips 新竹不是貢丸，貢丸是新竹的一項特色，故用 for。

例2 Hsinchu is famous as the Windy City.

新竹以風城聞名。

Tips 新竹就是風城，新竹有風城之稱，故用 as。

例3 David is famous for great teaching.

David 以卓越的教學聞名。

例4 David is famous as a good teacher.

David 以作為一位好老師而享有盛名。

例5 Jane is noted for her nice personality.

Jane 以她的好個性出名。

例6 Kevin is noted as a nice person.

Kevin 以身為好相處的人而出名。

練功坊

填空題

1. Tu Fu is noted ____ his poetry.

2. Mary is famous ____ an opera singer.

翻譯題

3. 臺灣以製造先進的電腦聞名。

_____

4. Mark 以做義工聞名。

38 be addicted to + N/V-ing　對…上癮
indulge in + N/V-ing　沉溺於…

說明

1. 注意上述句型表示「沉迷於…難以自拔」，通常帶有「因此蒙受其害」的負面句意。

2. 上述句型中的 to 和 in 都是介系詞，須接名詞或動名詞 (V-ing)。

例1 Jason has been addicted to playing online games for a long time.
Jason 已對玩線上遊戲上癮很久了。

例2 Jimmy is addicted to gambling, and his friends are worried about him.
Jimmy 迷上了賭博，他的朋友都為他擔心。

例3 Andy indulged in eating candy, so he had some decayed teeth.
Andy 很喜歡吃糖果，所以他有一些蛀牙。

句型比較

┌ be absorbed/immersed
│　　　　　　　　　　　　　 + in + N/V-ing
└ bury/immerse oneself

說明 上述句型表示「沉浸在…中」，用來強調非常喜歡某事，做得很專注，較無負面之意。

例1 Jeff was absorbed/immersed in his work and paid little attention to the outside world.

→ Jeff buried/immersed himself in his work and paid little attention to the outside world.
Jeff 專注於他的工作，不太注意外在的世界。

例2 Daniel was absorbed/immersed in his studies, trying to rank top in his class.

　　→ Daniel buried/immersed himself in his studies, trying to rank top in his class.

　　Daniel 專注於他的課業，設法在班上排名前面。

練功坊

翻譯題

1. Steve 酒精成癮，常常喝醉。

_____

2. Mark 沉溺於網購，常買一些不必要的東西。

_____

3. Fred 看電視看得很投入，沒注意到 Rick 來了。

_____

39

Instead of + N/V_1-ing..., S + V_2...
Rather than + N/V_1-ing/V_1..., S + V_2...
S + V_2...instead of + N/V_1-ing...
S + V_2...rather than + N/V_1-ing/V_1...　　作為⋯的替代

S + V_1...; instead, S + V_2...
S + V_1.... Instead/Rather, S + V_2...
S + V_1...; S + V_2...instead.

說明

1. 上述句型中的介系詞片語 instead of 可改成 rather than，接名詞或動名詞 (V-ing)。但 rather than 後還可以接原形動詞。

2. 上述句型中的 instead 若沒有馬上接 of，或是 rather 若沒有馬上接 than，則是 instead 或 rather 的副詞用法，此時須注意 instead 或 rather 在句中的位置，以及所搭配使用的分號或句號。

例1 He bought a used cellphone instead of a new one.

→ He bought a used cellphone <u>rather than</u> a new one.

他買了一支二手手機，而不是新手機。

[例2] John went to bed <u>instead of</u> doing his homework.

→ John went to bed <u>rather than</u> doing his homework.

→ John went to bed <u>rather than</u> do his homework.

→ <u>Instead of</u> doing his homework, John went to bed.

→ <u>Rather than</u> doing his homework, John went to bed.

→ <u>Rather than</u> do his homework, John went to bed.

→ John didn't do his homework; <u>instead</u>, he went to bed.

→ John didn't do his homework. <u>Instead/Rather</u>, he went to bed.

→ John didn't do his homework; he went to bed <u>instead</u>.

John 沒做作業，而是去睡覺。

[例3] Andy gives the poor a hand <u>instead of</u> ignoring them.

→ Andy gives the poor a hand <u>rather than</u> ignoring them.

→ Andy gives the poor a hand <u>rather than</u> ignore them.

→ <u>Instead of</u> ignoring the poor, Andy gives them a hand.

→ <u>Rather than</u> ignoring the poor, Andy gives them a hand.

→ <u>Rather than</u> ignore the poor, Andy gives them a hand.

→ Andy doesn't ignore the poor; <u>instead</u>, he gives them a hand.

→ Andy doesn't ignore the poor. <u>Instead/Rather</u>, he gives them a hand.

→ Andy doesn't ignore the poor; he gives them a hand <u>instead</u>.

Andy 對窮人伸出援手，而不是忽視他們。

✎ 練功坊

翻譯題

1. Steve 週末通常做運動，而非浪費時間打線上遊戲。

_____

2. 我喜歡吃夜市的小吃，而非在餐廳吃飯。

_____

40 lead to/contribute to/give rise to   導致⋯，造成⋯
result in/bring about

說明

1. 此句型中的 to 是介系詞。注意此句型原則上不可用於被動式。

2. 注意 result in (導致／造成⋯) 與 result from (起因於⋯) 的意思不同。

例1 Jack's success resulted from his hard work.

Jack 的成功起因於他的努力。

例2 Jack's hard work resulted in his success.

Jack 的努力帶來他的成功。

例3 Rick's laziness led to/contributed to/gave rise to/resulted in/brought about his failure.

Rick 的懶惰導致他的失敗。

例4 Serious corruption led to/contributed to/gave rise to/resulted in/brought about the fall of the great empire.

嚴重的貪汙造成這個偉大帝國的滅亡。

例5 Their ignorance of the law led to/contributed to/gave rise to/resulted in/brought about a great deal of trouble.

他們對法律的無知帶來很大的麻煩。

練功坊

翻譯題

1. 颱風造成山崩和水災。

2. 這場毀滅性的車禍導致道路封閉。

3. 嚴重乾旱造成食物短缺。

Chapter 7 　連接詞相關句型

41
$$S_1 + \begin{cases} \text{be..., and so + be} \\ \text{aux...., and so + aux.} \\ \text{V..., and so + do/does/did} \end{cases} + S_2 \quad \text{…也是…}$$

説明▶

此句型表示「…也是…」，如果是要表示「…也不…」，則將此句型中的 so 改成 nor 或 neither，其中 nor 前不需有 and。

例1 Angela is often late for school, and so is Ryan.
Angela 常上學遲到，Ryan 也是。

→ Angela is never late for school, and neither/nor is Ryan.
Angela 上學從不遲到，Ryan 也不。

例2 Mark will study abroad after graduation, and so will Paul.
Mark 畢業後要出國留學，Paul 也是。

→ Mark will not study abroad after graduation, and neither/nor will Paul.
Mark 畢業後不會出國留學，Paul 也不會。

例3 Dora checks her e-mail every day, and so does Lisa.
Dora 每天查看她的電子郵件，Lisa 也是。

→ Dora does not check her e-mail every day, and neither/nor does Lisa.
Dora 沒有每天查看她的電子郵件，Lisa 也沒有。

例4 Tom read the novel two days ago, and so did Mary.
Tom 兩天前讀了這本小說，Mary 也是。

→ Tom did not read the novel two days ago, and neither/nor did Mary.
Tom 兩天前沒有讀這本小說，Mary 也沒有。

✎練功坊

翻譯題

1. Nick 把書包放在書桌上，Betty 也是。

_____

2. Joseph 是個努力的學生，Linda 也是。

_____

3. 我不喜歡辣的食物，我妹妹也是。

_____

42 or, otherwise 否則

unless 除非

說明▶

1. or 和 unless 皆為連接詞，連接左右兩個句子。

2. otherwise 為副詞，須在其左邊加分號藉以連接左右兩個句子；或是獨立成一句，以句號隔開左右兩個句子。

例1 Apologize, or you will be sorry.

→ Apologize; otherwise, you will be sorry.

→ Apologize. Otherwise, you will be sorry.

道歉，否則你會遺憾。

💡Tips or 為連接詞，連接左右兩句。otherwise 為副詞，注意其用法。

例2 You will be sorry unless you apologize.

除非你道歉，不然你會遺憾。

→ You will be sorry if you don't apologize.

如果你不道歉，你會遺憾。

💡Tips unless 為連接詞。注意此句將 S + V...unless + S + V... 改寫為 S + V...if + S + aux. + not + V... 之後，語意略有變化。

練功坊

翻譯題

1. 你必須準時繳稅，否則會被罰。

_____

2. Rick 必需要在 11 點前回家，否則他會被媽媽處罰。

_____

3. 快點，否則我們可能會遲到。

_____

4. 除非我們快一點，不然我們可能會遲到。

_____

43

neither A nor B	非 A 也非 B
either A or B	不是 A 就是 B
A as well as B	A 和 B
both A and B	A 和 B 都
not only A (but) also B	不僅 A 而且 B

說明▶

上述句型須注意動詞的使用：

1. neither A nor B、either A or B、not only A (but) also B 這三組，其動詞的使用，由最靠近動詞的主詞來判斷。

2. A as well as B 由 A 來判斷其動詞的使用。

3. both A and B 由 A＋B 來判斷動詞的使用。

例1 Neither you nor <u>Tom</u> <u>is</u> qualified for the job.
　　你和 Tom 都無法勝任這項工作。

例2 Either you or <u>Tom</u> should take the responsibility.
　　不是你就是 Tom 應負起責任。

例3 Not only you but also <u>Tom</u> <u>is</u> qualified for the job.

不僅你而且 Tom 也適合這項工作。

〔例4〕You as well as Tom are qualified for the job.

你和 Tom 都適合這項工作。

〔例5〕Both you and Tom are qualified for the job.

你和 Tom 兩人都適合這項工作。

練功坊

〔翻譯題〕

1. Allen 不努力學習也不努力工作。

_____

2. 不是 Sandy 就是 Mary 會賽跑獲勝。

_____

3. 我們和 Joe 每天早上都去慢跑。

_____

4. 不僅 Steve 還有很多其他的學生在派對上玩得很愉快。

_____

44

{
As soon as + S + V...

The moment/instant/minute (that) + S + V...

Upon/On V-ing...

No sooner had + S + p.p....than + S + V-ed...
}

〔說明〕

上述句型表示「一…就…」，其中 Upon/On V-ing... 此一句型須注意，所省略的主詞須與主要子句的主詞一致。

〔例1〕Upon/On getting home, Fred turned on the TV.

Fred 一到家，就打開電視機。

🖉 Tips 前面所省略的主詞是 Fred，與主要子句的主詞 Fred 一致。

例2 As soon as/The moment/The instant/The minute the teacher came into the classroom, the students became quiet immediately.

→ No sooner had the teacher come into the classroom than the students became quiet immediately.

老師一走進教室，學生們立刻變安靜了。

Tips 此句因前後主詞不同，故不能用 Upon/On V-ing... 的句型。

例3 Right after I walked out of the house, I witnessed a traffic accident.

→ As soon as/The moment/The instant/The minute I walked out of the house, I witnessed a traffic accident.

→ Upon/On walking out of the house, I witnessed a traffic accident.

→ No sooner had I walked out of the house than I witnessed a traffic accident.

我一走出家門，就目擊一場車禍。

練功坊

翻譯題

1. 我一看到 Mary，什麼也沒說就走開了。

_____

2. 弟弟一聽到鬧鐘響就馬上跳下床。

_____

45 S + V₁ + so that/in order that + S + aux. + V₂　為了…

$$S + V_1 + \text{so that/in order that} + S + aux. + V_2$$

說明

so that 與 in order that 皆表示目的，意思是「為了…」。常用於此句型的助動詞有 may、will、can 等。

例1 I got up early so that I might see the sunrise.

→ I got up early in order that I might see the sunrise.

我為了能看到日出而早起。

例2 John came closer so that he could see the notice better.

→ John came closer in order that he could see the notice better.

John 靠近點以便可以更清楚地看那起告示。

句型比較

S + be/V + so + adj./adv. + that...

S + be/V + such + N + that...　　　　如此…以致於…

說明 注意第一個句型在 so 後面須接形容詞或副詞；第二個句型在 such 後面須接名詞或名詞片語。

例1 The report was well written. The teacher was pleased.

→ The report was so well written that the teacher was pleased.

→ It was such a well-written report that the teacher was pleased.

報告寫得很好，老師很高興。

Tips a well-written report (一份寫得很好的報告) 是名詞片語，接在 such 後面。

例2 Peter is so famous that everybody knows him.

→ Peter is such a famous person that everybody knows him.

Peter 很有名，每個人都認識他。

練功坊

翻譯題

1. Brad 搬家是為了能夠更靠近他的學校。

_____

2. 這位超級名模很漂亮又親切，很多人都喜歡她。

_____

46

Whether... (or not), S + V

Whether...or..., S + V

Whether + S + V₁ (or not) + be/V₂...

S + V + whether/if... (or not)

不管…；是否…

說明▶

1. 上述句型中的 or not 通常可以省略。

例句 Whether you like it (or not), I will tell you the truth.
不管你喜歡與否,我都要告訴你真相。

2. Whether...or..., S + V 為表示讓步的句型。

例句 Whether you will stay home or go out, you have to make the decision now.
不管你要待在家或外出,你現在就必須做決定。

3. Whether + S + V_1 (or not) + be/V_2... 為 whether 引導名詞子句當主詞的句型,whether + S + V_1 (or not) 為名詞子句,是整個句子的主詞。

例1 Whether Rick comes (or not) doesn't make any difference.
Rick 是否會來都沒什麼差別。

例2 It doesn't matter whether/if you win the game (or not).
不管你是否贏得這場比賽都沒關係。

　　🖎**Tips** 本例的 it 為虛主詞,真正的主詞為 whether 或 if 引導的名詞子句 whether/if you win the game (or not)。

4. S + V + whether/if... (or not) 則為 whether 或 if 引導名詞子句當受詞的句型。

例句 I don't know whether/if John has left Taiwan (or not).
我不知道 John 是否已經離開臺灣。

　　🖎**Tips** 此為 whether 引導的名詞子句當受詞的用法,在此 whether 可用 if 替換。

✎練功坊

翻譯題

1. 你來不來我的慶生會都無所謂。

_____

2. 不管你成功或失敗,我都會支持你。

_____

3. 不管你幫不幫我,我都會執行這個計畫。

_____

4. 我不確定我是否理解他的意思。

_____

47 Although/Though + S + V$_1$, S + V$_2$...
Despite/In spite of + the fact that + S + V$_1$, S + V$_2$...　　雖然…
Despite/In spite of/Notwithstanding + N/V$_1$-ing, S + V$_2$...

_____

說明▶

1. 上述句型切勿添加 but，以免連接詞過多。

2. although 和 though 為連接詞，所以可以馬上接子句；despite、in spite of 和 notwithstanding 則為介系詞，須先接 the fact that 才能接子句。

3. 第三個句型為介系詞接名詞或動名詞 (V-ing) 的用法，注意此句型須在前後主詞一致時才能使用。

例1 Although/Though he knew there were dangers ahead, he still went there.

　→ Despite/In spite of the fact that he knew there were dangers ahead, he still went there.

　→ Despite/In spite of/Notwithstanding knowing there were dangers ahead, he still went there.

雖然他知道前方有危險，他仍然去了那裡。

例2 Although/Though it was raining outside, the athletic meet still took place as scheduled.

　→ Despite/In spite of the fact that it was raining outside, the athletic meet still took place as scheduled.

雖然外面正在下雨，運動會仍然如期舉行。

Tips 本例前後主詞不一致，故不能用介系詞接名詞或動名詞 (V-ing) 的寫法。

✎ **練功坊**

翻譯題

1. 雖然他成績不好，他仍很努力學習。

_____

2. 儘管 Harry Brown 是個百萬富翁，他仍然努力工作。

_____

 48
$$\begin{cases} \text{(As) adj./adv. as + S + V}_1..., \text{S + V}_2... \\ \text{Although + S + V}_1..., \text{S + V}_2... \end{cases} \quad \text{雖然…，但是…}$$

說明▶

上述句型切勿再多加 but，以免連接詞過多。此一句型表示「雖然…，但是…」，可同時參考前面第 47 個句型的其他寫法。

例1 (As) fast as Fred ran, he still lost the race.

→ Although Fred ran fast, he still lost the race.

Fred 雖然跑得快，但還是輸掉了賽跑。

例2 (As) disabled as Josh was, he didn't lose his confidence.

→ Although Josh was disabled, he didn't lose his confidence.

雖然 Josh 殘障，但他並沒有失去自信。

例3 (As) poor as Kevin was, he still tried his best to help people in need.

→ Although Kevin was poor, he still tried his best to help people in need.

Kevin 雖然貧窮，但他仍盡力幫助有需要的人。

✎ **練功坊**

翻譯題

1. Ted 雖然注意聽，但他仍不懂老師在說什麼。

_____

2. 這老人雖然走得慢，但他仍然爬到了山頂。

_____

3. May 雖然一再失敗，但是她仍不放棄。

_____

49 $\begin{cases} \text{While} + S + V_1, S + V_2... \\ S + V_2...\text{while} + S + V_1... \end{cases}$ 當…；而…；雖然…

說明

while 有三個主要的意思，都常出現在大考當中：

1. 意思為「當…」時，後面常接進行式的子句，表示持續一段時間的動作。

例句 I was watching TV while Tom was sleeping in the room.

當 Tom 正在房間睡覺，我在看電視。

💡Tips while 所接的子句使用進行式 was sleeping。

2. 意思為「而…」時，常出現的用法為 some...while some/others... (有些…而有些…)。

例句 Some students enjoy playing online games while others like reading comic books in their free time.

有些學生喜愛玩線上遊戲，而有些學生喜歡在空閒時看漫畫。

3. 意思為「雖然…」時常放在句首，用法類似 although 和 though。

例1 While Alex is short, he is an outstanding player in the school basketball team.

→ Although/Though Alex is short, he is an outstanding player in the school basketball team.

雖然 Alex 很矮，他是學校籃球隊中的傑出球員。

💡Tips 這裡的 while 可以替換成 although 或 though。

例2 While Rick failed many times, he never gave up.

→ Although/Though Rick failed many times, he never gave up.

Rick 雖然失敗多次，但他從沒放棄。

練功坊

翻譯題

1. 當我在湖邊慢跑時，Mark 在釣魚。

_____

2. 我媽媽喜歡逛街，而我爸爸喜歡待在家。

_____

3. 雖然在下雨，我們還是決定去野餐。

_____

50
$\begin{cases} \text{Because} + S + V_1..., S + V_2... \\ \dfrac{\text{Because of/As a result of/}}{\text{Owing to/Due to}} + \text{N/V-ing, S + V...} \end{cases}$ 由於；因為

說明

because 是連接詞，後面須接子句；because of、as a result of、owing to 或 due to 是介系詞，後面須接名詞或動名詞 (V-ing)。

例1 Sarah did not show up at the wedding because she had a high fever.
Sarah 沒出現在婚宴上，因為她發高燒。

例2 Because of/As a result of/Owing to/Due to lack of timely help, the poor man got drowned in the river.
由於缺乏及時的協助，那個可憐的男人在河裡溺斃了。

例3 Life there was difficult because of/as a result of/owing to/due to shortage of water.
因為缺水，那裡的生活很艱困。

例4 Morgan sold his house because of/as a result of/owing to/due to financial difficulties.
Morgan 因為財務困難而賣掉他的房子。

句型比較

Thanks to + N/V$_1$-ing, S + V$_2$...　幸虧⋯

說明 thanks to 是介系詞，後面須接名詞或動名詞 (V-ing)。

例1 Thanks to my parents' encouragement, I finally completed my thesis.
　　幸虧有我爸媽的鼓勵，我終於完成我的論文。

例2 Thanks to Mike's help, I finally finished the hard task and felt relieved.
　　幸虧 Mike 幫忙，我終於完成這項困難的任務，並且感到放心。

 練功坊

翻譯題

1. 由於 Joe 的懶散，他英文和數學都不及格。

_____

2. 因為我已經三個月沒領到薪水了，所以我辭掉工作。

_____

3. 幸虧有他的體諒，我鬆了一口氣。

_____

51

$\begin{cases} \text{Because/Since} + S + V_1..., S + V_2... \\ S + V_2...\text{because/since/for} + S + V_1... \end{cases}$　因為⋯

說明

上述句型中的三個連接詞皆有 「因為⋯」 的意思，後面須接子句。 其中 because 和 since 置於句中或句首都可以；但 for 只能置於句中，不可放在句首，而且此時的 for 通常會在前面加上逗號。

例1 The little boy cried because he was scolded by his mom.

→ The little boy cried since he was scolded by his mom.

→ The little boy cried, for he was scolded by his mom.

小男孩因為被媽媽責罵所以哭了。

[例2] Because Jeff has been working hard, he got promoted last week.

→ Since Jeff has been working hard, he got promoted last week.

→ Jeff got promoted last week, for he has been working hard.

Jeff 因為一直很努力工作所以上週升職了。

練功坊

選擇題

(　　) 1. We stayed at home ＿＿＿ the bad weather.

(A) because　　　(B) since　　　(C) for　　　(D) because of

(　　) 2. ＿＿＿ a lot of students didn't pay attention in class, the teacher got mad and stopped helping students review the lessons. (複選)

(A) Because　　　(B) Since　　　(C) For　　　(D) Because of

翻譯題

3. 因為在下雨，交通變得更糟了。

_____

4. 表演者因為沒有觀眾而感到沮喪。

_____

52 S + V₁..., 數量詞 + of <u>whom/which</u> + V₂...

$$S + V_1..., 數量詞 + of \underline{whom/which} + V_2...$$

說明▶

此種句型是為去掉連接詞與代名詞，而由關係代名詞取代，因關係代名詞有連接詞與代名詞的功能。關係代名詞用 whom 代替人，用 which 代替物。

例1 I have six sisters, and two of them are nurses.

→ I have six sisters, two of whom are nurses.

我有六個姊姊，其中兩個是護士。

Tips 連接詞 and 和代名詞 them，由關係代名詞 whom 取代。因為 of 是介系詞，而本句的關係代名詞所指為人，故用受格 whom。

例2 I have nine books, and three of them are about gardening.

→ I have nine books, three of which are about gardening.

我有九本書，其中三本是關於園藝的。

Tips 連接詞 and 和代名詞 them，由關係代名詞 which 取代。因為 of 是介系詞，而本句的關係代名詞所指為物，故用受格 which。

例3 I have three new bikes, and all of them are made in Taiwan.

→ I have three new bikes, all of which are made in Taiwan.

我有三輛新的腳踏車，全都是在臺灣製造的。

例4 I have a lot of foreign friends, and some of them are from Japan.

→ I have a lot of foreign friends, some of whom are from Japan.

我有很多外國朋友，其中一些來自日本。

練功坊

選擇題

(　　) 1. A lot of students went camping. Some of ____ got lost.

　　(A) whom　　　(B) which　　　(C) them　　　(D) who

(　　) 2. Ten million tourists come to Taiwan for sightseeing every year, one million of ____ are from Japan.

(A) them　　　(B) which　　　(C) whom　　　(D) whose

(　) 3. There are a large number of people speaking Mandarin, ____ can also speak Taiwanese.

(A) and many of them

(B) many of them

(C) and many of whom

(D) many of who

(　) 4. David wrote eight books, two of ____ were about English grammar.

(A) which　　　(B) them　　　(C) whom　　　(D) it

翻譯題

5. 我看到很多馬拉松跑者，其中一些來自肯亞 (Kenya)。

---

53 $\begin{cases} \text{What} \\ \text{All (that)} \end{cases}$ + S + have/need to do is (to) + V...　…所必須做的就是…

說明▶

此句型 is 後的 to 都省略，故會出現 is + V，看似文法不正確，但其實為正確的句子。

例1 What/All (that) Alex has to do is (to) concentrate on his work.

Alex 所必須要做的就是專心在他的工作上。

例2 What/All (that) a teacher needs to do is (to) teach well and care about students.

老師所必須要做的是好好教書，並關心學生。

例3 What/All (that) you have to do is (to) obey the laws and be a good citizen.

你所必須要做的是遵守法律，並且當個好公民。

練功坊

翻譯題

1. Kevin 必須做的是節食且持續運動。

_____

2. 市長必須做的是讓市政府運作得更好。

_____

3. 我爸爸每天在家必須做的是打掃屋子和煮晚餐。

_____

54
...whoever...		…不論什麼人…
...whomever...	+ (S) + V...	…不論什麼人…
...whichever...		…不論哪一種／個…
...whatever...		…不論什麼事／東西…

說明

1. whoever = anyone who 當主格用；whomever = anyone whom 當受格用。

例1 My uncle will give a new bike to whoever (= anyone who) passes the exam in my family.

我叔叔將送一部新單車給我家族中任何通過考試的人。

Tips whoever 在此當主詞，passes 為動詞。

例2 Whomever (= Anyone whom) my mom invited for dinner could bring a gift home.

任何被我媽媽邀請來吃晚餐的人都可以帶個禮物回家。

Tips whomever 在此當 invited 的受詞，故用受格。

2. whichever = any/either of which 當主格或受格用 ；whatever = anything that 當主格或受格用。

例1 Here are a cake and a biscuit roll. You can take whichever (= any/either of which) you want.

這裡有蛋糕和蛋捲。你可以拿任何你想要的。

🔦**Tips** whichever 在此當作 want 的受詞作受格用。

〔例2〕 Whatever (= Anything that) is done by Will is well done.

Will 所做的任何事都做得很好。

🔦**Tips** whatever 在此當主詞作主格用。

〔例3〕 Since you are my best friend, I will support whatever (= anything that) you decide to do.

因為你是我最好的朋友，不論你決定要做什麼事我都會支持。

🔦**Tips** whatever 在此當 decide to do 的受詞作受格用。

✎ 練功坊

翻譯題

1. 任何認識 Rick 的人都知道他來自這個南美小國。

_____

2. 我不喜歡任何總是遲到的人。

_____

3. 在這四本書中，你可以拿任何一本你喜歡的。

_____

55

$$S + V + \begin{cases} \text{the very} \\ \text{the only} \\ \text{the same} \end{cases} + N + that...$$

說明▶

that 在此為關係代名詞，先行詞前有 the very、the only 或 the same，則關係代名詞通常用 that。

〔例句〕 This is the very book that I am looking for.

我在找的正是這本書。

🔦**Tips** 先行詞 book 前有 the very，所以關係代名詞用 that。

句型比較

S + V + anything/nothing/everything/something + that...

說明 先行詞為 anything、nothing、everything 或 something 時，關係代名詞通常也是用 that。

例句 The doctor said he would do everything that he could to save patients' lives.
這位醫生說他會盡他所能來挽救病人的生命。

🔖Tips 先行詞為 everything，所以關係代名詞用 that。

 練功坊

翻譯題

1. 《星際大戰》(*Star Wars*) 是我看過最好看的電影。

_____

2. Jason 買過最貴的腳踏車是新臺幣 25,000 元。

_____

56 The idea/fact/belief/thought that S + V$_1$... + V$_2$...
S + V$_1$ + the idea/fact/belief/thought that S + V$_2$...

說明

用一個句子當主詞時，或是在介系詞後加一個句子時，可用上述方式以 that 引導名詞子句。

例1 The thought that he wanted to work part-time really shocked me.
他想要去打工的想法真的令我很震驚。

🔖Tips he wanted to work part-time 不能直接當主詞，前面加上 the thought that 成為名詞子句後才可當主詞。the thought 指的就是 he wanted to work part-time。

例2 I was not interested in the fact that Mary married her boss.
我對 Mary 嫁給她老闆一事不感興趣。

🔖Tips 介系詞後不可直接加句子 Mary married her boss，加上 the fact that 使它變成名詞子句就可以接在介系詞後。the fact 指的就是 Mary married her boss。

例3 I hold the belief that love conquers all. 我抱持著愛會征服一切的信念。

🔍**Tips** the belief 指的就是 love conquers all。

練功坊

翻譯題

1. 他是個美國人這個事實讓我很驚訝。

_____

2. 我對於奶奶好起來了這個事實感到高興。

_____

3. 全球化造成更多問題這個想法似乎是對的。

_____

 57 ...wh- + S + V　(名詞子句)

說明▶

此為疑問詞引導的名詞子句，作句中主詞、受詞、或補語的用法。疑問詞如 what、who、when、where、why、how 或 if 及 whether 可有這個用法。這樣的名詞子句特別要注意其主詞和動詞的先後順序應如下排列：wh- + 主詞 + 動詞。

例1 What Rick said is not true.

Rick 所說的不是真的。

🔍**Tips** what Rick said 為名詞子句，由疑問詞 what + 主詞 Rick + 動詞 said 所組成，整個名詞子句當全句的主詞。

例2 Rick is not what he was.

Rick 不是以前的他了。

🔍**Tips** what he was 當主詞補語，補充說明主詞 Rick。

例3 I don't know where Rick lives.

我不知道 Rick 住哪裡。

🔍**Tips** where Rick lives 當 know 的受詞。

例4 Peter doesn't tell me what he will do.

Peter 沒有告訴我他將會做什麼。

🔎Tips 本句中的 tell 須接兩個受詞：me 為 tell 的間接受詞，而名詞子句 what he will do
則是 tell 的直接受詞。

例5 Daniel really doesn't know what he should do.

→ Daniel really doesn't know what to do.

Daniel 真的不知道他該做什麼。

🔎Tips 本句中的 wh- + S + V 當受詞，可改成 wh- + to + V。

例6 I really don't know whether I should trust Andy or not.

→ I really don't know whether to trust Andy or not.

我真的不知道我是否應該相信 Andy。

🔎Tips 本句中的 wh- + S + V 當受詞，可改成 wh- + to + V。

✏練功坊

翻譯題

1. 我不相信 Helen 所說過的事。

_____

2. 我對於 Alex 是如何認識他的女朋友感到很有興趣。

_____

3. 你吃什麼就是什麼。

_____

Chapter 9　虛主詞與虛受詞相關句型

58

$$It + \begin{cases} \text{occurs to sb.} \\ \text{strikes sb.} \\ \text{dawns on sb.} \end{cases} + that + S + V... \quad (突然) 想起…，意識到…$$

說明▶

It 在上述句型中為虛主詞，真主詞為其後之 that 子句。

[例1] On my way to school, it occurred to me that I forgot to take my wallet.

→ On my way to school, it struck me that I forgot to take my wallet.

→ On my way to school, it dawned on me that I forgot to take my wallet.

在我上學途中，我想起我忘了帶錢包。

[例2] It never occurred to me that Jack was a thief.

→ It never struck me that Jack was a thief.

→ It never dawned on me that Jack was a thief.

我從沒想到 Jack 是個小偷。

練功坊

翻譯題

1. 我今早想到我今天不用上學。

_____

2. Tim 突然想到他需要帶他媽媽去看醫生。

_____

3. Fred 突然想起他已經兩年沒見到他的表哥了。

_____

59

It is not surprising that + S + V...
It comes as no surprise that + S + V...　…一點都不讓人驚訝
Unsurprisingly, S + V...

說明▶

上述句型中的 it 為虛主詞，真主詞為後面的 that 子句。副詞 unsurprisingly 修飾其後的整個句子。此句型可簡單地套用在作文中。

例1 It was not surprising that Tom won first place in the English speech contest.

→ It came as no surprise that Tom won first place in the English speech contest.

→ Unsurprisingly, Tom won first place in the English speech contest.

Tom 贏得英文演講比賽第一名一點也不讓人驚訝。

例2 It was not surprising that Patrick, a genius, graduated from college at the age of 18.

→ It came as no surprise that Patrick, a genius, graduated from college at the age of 18.

→ Unsurprisingly, Patrick, a genius, graduated from college at the age of 18.

Patrick 這位天才 18 歲從大學畢業一點也不讓人驚訝。

練功坊

翻譯題

1. 我弟，一位懶散的學生，沒通過考試一點也不讓人驚訝。

_____

2. Johnny，又高又帥，變成超級名模，一點也不讓人驚訝。

_____

60
$$\begin{cases} \text{It is likely that} + S + V... \\ S + \text{be likely to} + V... \end{cases}$$ 可能…

說明

此一句型用來表示可能會發生的事，it 為虛主詞，真主詞為其後的 that 子句。likely 是形容詞，意思是「可能的」。而 that 子句中的主詞不限，可以是人、事或物。

例1 It is likely that Hazel will run for president again.

→ Hazel is likely to run for president again.

Hazel 可能再一次競選總統。

例2 It is likely that the minister will resign due to the low approval rating.

→ The minister is likely to resign due to the low approval rating.

這位部長有可能因支持率低而辭職。

例3 James is more likely to win his second MVP award this year.

James 更有可能在今年贏得他的第二個最有價值球員獎。

Tips be more likely to 接原形動詞，意思為「更有可能…」。

例4 It is cloudy now, and it is more likely to rain this afternoon.

現在是陰天，下午更有可能下雨。

練功坊

翻譯題

1. Josh 下個月有可能搬去臺南。

_____

2. Sarah 這週末有可能去爬山。

_____

3. Lily 明年有可能買新房子。

_____

61

$$\text{It is} + \begin{cases} \text{important (重要的)/} \\ \text{vital (極重要的)/} \\ \text{crucial (至關重要的)/} \\ \text{critical (關鍵性的)/} \\ \text{necessary (必需的)/} \\ \text{essential (必要的)} \end{cases} + \text{that} + S + (\text{should}) + V$$

說明

以上這些形容詞常以 it 為虛主詞，後面加上 that 子句當真主詞；子句中常用 should 後接原形動詞，其中的 should 可以省略。

例1 It is vital that Dad (should) work hard to support our family.
我爸爸努力工作賺錢養家是很重要的。

例2 It is necessary that Mary (should) get up at 6:00 in the morning.
Mary 在早上六點起床是必需的。

例3 It is important that every student (should) pay attention in class.
每個學生專心上課是重要的。

練功坊

翻譯題

1. 駕駛開車時注意交通號誌是必要的。

_____

2. 人應該保護環境，這是至關重要的。

_____

3. 你要控制體重，這很重要。

_____

4. 學生準時上學是必需的。

_____

62
$$\begin{cases} \text{It seems/seemed that} + S + V \\ S + \text{seem/seemed to} + \begin{cases} V \\ \text{have} + p.p. \end{cases} \quad \text{似乎…} \end{cases}$$

說明

上述句型須注意其過去式的動詞變化。第一個句型的 that 子句若是在敘述過去或已發生很久的事，改成第二個句型時，則用 to + have + p.p.。

例1 It seems that Helen is a beauty.

→ Helen seems to be a beauty. Helen 似乎是個美女。

例2 It seemed that Helen was a beauty.

→ Helen seemed to have been a beauty. Helen 以前似乎是個美女。

Tips 「似乎」與「過去似乎」之用法不同，須注意搭配不同的動詞時態。

例3 It seems that the Lin family has lived in the U.S. for a long time.

→ The Lin family seems to have lived in the U.S. for a long time.

林家人似乎在美國住很久了。

Tips 本例為「似乎已發生很久的事」之用法。

例4 It seemed that Rick had a bad cold.

→ Rick seemed to have had a bad cold. Rick 似乎得了重感冒。

例5 It seems that Steve is a high school teacher.

→ Steve seems to be a high school teacher. Steve 似乎是個中學老師。

練功坊

翻譯題

1. Alex 似乎是個網球好手。

_____

2. Daniel 似乎犯了大錯。

_____

3. 他們似乎一起工作很久了。

_____

63
$$\begin{cases} \text{It is + adj. + for sb. + to V} \\ \text{To V + is + adj. + for sb.} \quad \text{做…對某人是…} \\ \text{V-ing + is + adj. + for sb.} \end{cases}$$

說明 ▶

It is + adj. + for sb. + to V 為常用句型，it 為虛主詞，真主詞為後面的不定詞。

例句 It is important for students to study harder before the midterm.

　→ To study harder before the midterm is important for students.

　→ Studying harder before the midterm is important for students.

期中考前更加用功對學生是重要的。

句型比較 ▶

S + be + too + adj. + to V　太…而無法…

說明 too... + to V 這個句型帶有否定意味。

例1 Grace is too busy to have time for lunch.

Grace 太忙而沒有時間吃午餐。

例2 It is never too late to learn.

學習永遠不嫌晚。

練功坊

翻譯題

1. 對你而言，30 分鐘內跑完 5 公里很容易。

_____

2. Allen 太害羞而無法公開演說。

_____

3. 對 Bob 而言，現在道歉已經太遲了。

_____

64 Rumor/Legend has it that + S + V...　謠傳／傳說…

說明

此句型中的 rumor 或 legend 不必加冠詞，it 為虛受詞，真受詞為後面的 that 子句。

例1 Rumor has it that the player will be traded.

謠傳那位球員將被交易。

例2 Legend has it that Liao Tian-ding robbed the rich and helped the poor.

傳說廖添丁劫富濟貧。

句型比較

┌ It is said that + S + V...

└ People/They say that + S + V...　　聽說…

說明 It is said... 為被動句型；People/They say... 則為主動句型。

例1 It is said that the actress will marry a rich businessman.

→ People/They say that the actress will marry a rich businessman.

聽說那位女演員將嫁給一位富商。

例2 It is said that David has a high IQ.

→ People/They say that David has a high IQ.

聽說 David 有很高的智商。

✎ 練功坊

翻譯題

1. 謠傳 Mary 對她老公不忠。

_____

2. 聽說部長很快就會辭職。

_____

3. 傳說山洞裡面住著一對夫婦。

_____

65 S + $\begin{cases} \text{make (使得)/find (覺得)} \\ \text{consider/think (認為)} \end{cases}$ + it + adj./N + (for sb.) + to V

說明

此句型中的 it 為虛受詞，真正的受詞是不定詞。

例1 Airplanes make it easier for people to travel around the world.

飛機使得人們環遊世界更簡單。

⚘Tips 真正的受詞為 to travel around the world。

例2 The athletes think it unfair for them to compete in the rain.

運動員們認為對他們而言在雨中比賽不公平。

⚘Tips 真正的受詞為 to compete in the rain。

例3 Joe found it interesting to read stories to children.

Joe 覺得念故事給孩子們聽是很有趣的事。

例4 Peter considered it difficult to live in Alaska in the harsh winter.

Peter 認為在嚴冬時節很難在阿拉斯加生活。

例5 Steve thought it immoral to make fake news.

Steve 認為製造假新聞是不道德的。

例6 Joseph thought it a privilege to eat in the VIP room.

Joseph 認為在貴賓室吃飯是種殊榮。

練功坊

翻譯題

1. 外面巨大的噪音讓學生上課很難專心。

_____

2. Andy 覺得每週打工三次很累人。

_____

3. Helen 認為花時間精通一種外語很值得。

_____

Chapter 10　假設用法相關句型

66 If + S + were/V-ed..., S + would/might/could/should + V...

　　 If + S + had + p.p...., S + would/might/could/should + have + p.p....

說明

1. If + S + were/V-ed..., S + would/might/could/should + V... 表示與現在事實相反的假設。

 If + S + had + p.p...., S + would/might/could/should + have + p.p.... 表示與過去事實相反的假設。

2. 在假設語氣句型中須特別注意，與現在事實相反的假設，不論人稱，be 動詞一律用 were，不用 was。

例1 If I had enough money, I would buy a new sports car.
如果我有足夠的錢，我就買一部新的跑車。

　Tips 本例為與現在事實相反的假設。 事實是 I do not have enough money now, so I cannot buy a new sports car.。

例2 If I were a teacher, I would give my students less homework.
→ Were I a teacher, I would give my students less homework.
如果我是老師，我會給學生少一點作業。

　Tips 本例為與現在事實相反的假設。本例可將 if 去掉，並將 were 移至句首，形成倒裝句。事實是 I am not a teacher, so I do not give students less homework.。

例3 If I had been a teacher then, I would have given my students less homework.
→ Had I been a teacher then, I would have given my students less homework.
如果當時我是老師，我就給學生少一點作業。

　Tips 本例為與過去事實相反的假設。本例可將 if 去掉，並將 had 移至句首，形成倒裝句。事實是 I was not a teacher then, so I did not give students less homework.。

例4 If I had had a bachelor's degree, I would have found a better job.
→ Had I had a bachelor's degree, I would have found a better job.
如果當時我有學士學位，我就能找到更好的工作。

🔧Tips 本例為與過去事實相反的假設。事實是 I did not have a bachelor's degree, so I did not find a better job.。

✎練功坊

翻譯題

1. 如果我每天多運動，我就會變得更有活力。

_____

2. 如果 Tom 去年多用功一點，他就能進入一所較好的大學。

_____

67
⎧ If it were not for + N, S + could/might/would/should + V
⎨ Were it not for + N, S + could/might/would/should + V
⎩
⎧ If it had not been for + N, S + could/might/would/should + have + p.p.
⎨ Had it not been for + N, S + could/might/would/should + have + p.p.
⎩
要不是⋯

說明▶

這些句型皆有假設的意味，中文意思為「要不是⋯」。

1. If it were/Were it not for + N, S + could/might/would/should + V 用於描述現在，為與現在事實相反的假設語氣。

2. If it had/Had it not been for + N, S + could/might/would/should + have + p.p. 用於描述過去，為與過去事實相反的假設語氣。

例1 If it were not for Ted's help, I could not finish the work on time.

　→ Were it not for Ted's help, I could not finish the work on time.
　要不是有 Ted 的幫忙，我不可能準時完成工作。

例2 If it were not for Mary's praise, I might not have confidence in myself.

　→ Were it not for Mary's praise, I might not have confidence in myself.
　要不是有 Mary 的讚美，我可能不會對自己有信心。

例3 If it had not been for Dad's financial support then, I could not have formed the company.

→ Had it not been for Dad's financial support then, I could not have formed the company.

當時要不是有爸爸的財務協助，我不可能成立公司。

例4 If it had not been for Bob's apology, I would not have forgiven him.

→ Had it not been for Bob's apology, I would not have forgiven him.

要不是 Bob 有道歉，我不會原諒他。

練功坊

翻譯題

1. 要不是我的勸告，Daniel 可能會再次犯下這個錯誤。

_____

2. 當時要不是我老師的建議，我可能會主修數學。

_____

3. 要不是去年成功的手術，Alex 可能已經死了。

_____

68 S + wish + (that) + 子句　　…但願…
S + wish + O + N...　　…祝福…
S + wish + to V...　　…想要…

說明

1. wish + (that) + 子句表示「但願…」，that 可省略，此一句型帶有假設意味。that 後面的子句若用過去式，表示與現在事實不符；若用過去完成式，則表示與過去事實不符。

例1 I wish (that) I were a bird.

但願我是隻鳥。

 Tips 「我不可能是鳥」，可知本例要表示的為與現在事實不符，故用過去式。注意與現在事實相反的假設語氣，不論主詞為何，be 動詞一律用 were，不可用 was。

〔例2〕 I wish (that) I had been to Africa last year.

但願去年我去過非洲。

🌟Tips 此為與過去事實不符，表示「去年我沒去非洲」，故用過去完成式 had + p.p.。

〔例3〕 Maggie wishes (that) she could have studied abroad.

Maggie 但願她有出國留學。

2. wish + O + N 表示「祝福…」，受詞後面須接名詞。

〔例1〕 I wish you a happy birthday.

我祝你生日快樂。

🌟Tips a happy birthday 為名詞，接在受詞 you 後面。

〔例2〕 I wish you good luck.

我祝你好運。

3. S + wish + to V 表示「想要…」。

〔例1〕 I wish to buy a new laptop next month.

下個月我想買一部新筆電。

〔例2〕 I wish to visit the Eiffel Tower next year.

明年我想去參觀艾菲爾鐵塔。

✏️練功坊

翻譯題

1. 但願我去年能買部新車。

_____

2. 但願我有足夠的時間去做我想做的事。

_____

3. 我祝我父母身體健康。

_____

69 { It's (high) time + for sb. + to V...
　　 　It's (high) time + that + S + V-ed...　　該是…的時候了

說明

此一句型帶有假設意味，表示期望發生但事實上還未發生的事，故 that 後面的子句用過去式。

例1 It's (high) time for us to work together.

→ It's (high) time that we worked together.

該是我們攜手努力的時候了。

例2 It is (high) time for us, seniors in high school, to study hard.

→ It is (high) time that we, seniors in high school, studied hard.

該是我們高三生好好用功讀書的時候了。

練功坊

翻譯題

1. 該是 Tom 說實話的時候了。

_____

2. 該是總統做正確抉擇的時候了。

_____

3. 該是我們交作業的時候了。

_____

Chapter 11　否定用法相關句型

$$S + \begin{cases} \text{no} \\ \text{not} \\ \text{never} \end{cases} + V_1 + \text{without} + N/V_2\text{-ing} \quad 沒有…就不…；每次都…$$

70

說明

no/not/never 加上 without 成為雙重否定，中譯為「沒有…就不能…」，意味著「有…就能…」、「每次都…」。

例1 A typhoon does not come without causing losses.
每次颱風來都會造成損失。

例2 Bob never visits me without bringing a gift to me.
Bob 每次來看我都會帶個禮物給我。

句型比較

┌ S + would not be complete without + N/V-ing　沒有…就不完整
└ No.../Nothing would be complete without + N/V-ing　有…才完整

說明 此為雙重否定，翻譯時須注意語意轉換。without 為介系詞，後面須接名詞或動名詞 (V-ing)。

例1 My birthday party would not be complete without a birthday cake.
沒有生日蛋糕，我的慶生會就不完整。

例2 Our graduation trip would not be complete without visiting Taroko Gorge.
如果沒去太魯閣，我們的畢業旅行就不圓滿了。

例3 No reunion would be complete without having a feast.
團聚要吃頓大餐才完整。

練功坊

翻譯題

1. Joe 每次來臺南都會來拜訪我。

_____

2. 沒有健康就沒有幸福。

_____

3. 沒去迪士尼樂園玩,這趟旅行就不圓滿。

_____

71
$$\begin{cases} \text{It can't be denied that + S + V...} \\ \text{There is no denying that + S + V...} \quad 不可否認的\cdots \\ \text{No one can deny that + S + V...} \end{cases}$$

說明

此句型的重點在於 deny 的變化,應注意何時用 denied、denying 或 deny。

例1 It can't be denied that Korean soap operas are popular in Taiwan.

→ There is no denying that Korean soap operas are popular in Taiwan.

→ No one can deny that Korean soap operas are popular in Taiwan.

無可否認的,韓劇在臺灣很受歡迎。

例2 It can't be denied that David is a good teacher.

→ There is no denying that David is a good teacher.

→ No one can deny that David is a good teacher.

無可否認的,David 是位好老師。

練功坊

翻譯題

1. 不可否認的,勤勞是成功的關鍵。

_____

2. 不可否認的，健康重於一切。

_____

3. 不可否認的，教育是非常強而有力的武器。

_____

72

$$\text{S + } \underline{\text{cannot}}/\underline{\text{can't}}/\underline{\text{can never}} + \begin{cases} \text{be + too + adj.} \\ \text{V (+ O) + too + adv.} \end{cases} \quad \text{再…也不為過}$$

說明

此一句型須注意正確理解其句意。助動詞 can 後接否定字詞，搭配後面的 too，用來表示「再…也不為過」或「愈…愈好」。此一句型亦可作下列形式的改寫：

$$\text{S + } \underline{\text{cannot}}/\underline{\text{can't}}/\underline{\text{can never}} + \begin{bmatrix} \text{be + adj. + enough} \\ \text{V (+ O) + adv. + enough} \end{bmatrix}$$

例1 The coach cannot/can't/can never be too strict when leading the national team.

→ The coach cannot/can't/can never be strict enough when leading the national team.

這位教練帶領國家代表隊，再怎麼嚴格也不為過。

例2 One cannot/can't/can never be too cautious about choosing a job.

→ One cannot/can't/can never be cautious enough about choosing a job.

一個人在選擇職業上，再怎麼仔細考慮也不為過。

例3 The company cannot/can't/can never act too cautiously when it comes to making new regulations.

→ The company cannot/can't/can never act cautiously enough when it comes to making new regulations.

公司要制訂新的規章制度時，再怎麼謹慎行事也不為過。

練功坊

翻譯題

1. 父母在照顧小孩這件事上，再怎麼謹慎也不為過。

_____

2. 你在提款時，再怎麼仔細檢查你的帳戶也不為過。

_____

73

$$S + V_1..., \begin{cases} \text{not to mention} \\ \text{not to speak of} \\ \text{to say nothing of} \end{cases} + V_2\text{-ing...}$$

更不用說

$$S + V_1..., \begin{cases} \text{let alone} \\ \text{much less} \end{cases} + V_2...$$

說明

1. not to mention/not to speak of/to say nothing of + V-ing 可用來表示肯定及否定的句子；而 let alone/much less + V 僅能用來表示否定的句子。

2. 肯定用法表示逗點前後所提到的事情都會做；而否定用法表示逗點前後所提到的事情都不會做。

例1 David can drive a bus, not to mention/not to speak of/to say nothing of (driving) a car.

David 會開公車，更不用說小汽車了。

Tips 本例逗點前的主要子句為肯定句，代表有能力做逗點前後所提到的兩種事情，此時不能以 let alone/much less + V 改寫本例。

例2 David can't drive a car, not to mention/not to speak of/to say nothing of (driving) a bus.

→ David can't drive a car, let alone/much less (drive) a bus.

David 不會開小汽車，更不用說公車了。

Tips 本例逗點前的主要子句為否定句，代表沒有能力做逗點前後所提到的兩種事情，此時可用 let alone/much less + V 改寫本例。

例3 Maggie can lift a heavy desk, not to mention/not to speak of/to say nothing of moving the light box.

Maggie 能舉起一個沉重的書桌，更不用說搬動這個輕箱子。

例4 Helen could not read English, not to mention/not to speak of/to say nothing of writing in English.

→ Helen could not read English, let alone/much less write in English.

Helen 看不懂英文，更不用說用英文寫作了。

練功坊

翻譯題

1. Jane 會騎機車，更不用說腳踏車。

_____

2. 這位老人不能走路，更不用說跑步。

_____

3. 這位婦人無法舉起這個小箱子，更不用說這張大書桌。

_____

74

$$\text{Not only} + \begin{cases} \text{aux.} + \text{S} + \text{V}... \\ \text{be} + \text{S}... \end{cases}, \text{but} + \text{S} + \begin{cases} \text{also} + \text{V} \\ \text{be...also...} \\ \text{aux.} + \text{also} + \text{V}... \end{cases} \quad 不僅…而且…$$

Not until... + aux. + S + V...　直到…才…

說明

not only 與 not until 帶有否定意味，放在句首有強調的作用，須用倒裝。倒裝時主詞與動詞的順序要對換。

例1 Not until recently were they able to confirm which genes in the DNA cause those diseases.

直到最近，他們才能夠證實是 DNA 裡的哪些基因造成那些疾病。

> 💡**Tips** 句首為否定詞 not until，所以須用倒裝句型，故將動詞移到主詞前，形成 were they able...。

例2 Not only did Bob go jogging, but he also played tennis twice a week.

Bob 不僅慢跑，而且還每週打網球兩次。

句型補充

$$\left.\begin{array}{l} \text{Little (很少)/Seldom (很少)/} \\ \text{Hardly (幾乎不)/Rarely (幾乎不)/} \\ \text{Never (絕不)/By no means (絕不)/} \\ \text{Only (僅)} \end{array}\right\} + \begin{cases} \text{aux.} + \text{S} + \text{V}... \\ \text{be} + \text{S}... \end{cases}$$

說明 little、seldom、hardly、rarely、never、by no means、only 等在上述句型中皆為否定副詞的用法，放在句首時有強調的作用，也須用倒裝，將主詞與動詞的順序對換。

例1 Never did I have the chance to go to college when I was young.

我年輕時從未有機會上大學。

> 💡**Tips** 句首為否定副詞 never，所以須用倒裝句型，故將助動詞移到主詞前，形成 did I have...。

例2 Little did he know what had happened to his brother.
他不太知道他弟弟發生了什麼事。

例3 By no means is he a person you can trust.
他絕不是一個你可以信賴的人。

練功坊

翻譯題

1. 她很少吃粥或飯當早餐。(請以否定詞為句首)

_____

2. Alex 幾乎沒時間休息,因為他太忙了。(請以否定詞為句首)

_____

75 地方副詞 + 代名詞 + 動詞
地方副詞 + 動詞 + 名詞

說明

此為地方副詞置於句首的倒裝句,可利用四字口訣「代動,動名」來幫助記憶順序。

例1 She stood in front of the building.

→ In front of the building she stood.
她站在大樓前面。

💡Tips she 為代名詞,搭配口訣可知倒裝的順序應為:地方副詞 + 代 + 動,所以代名詞 she 要放在動詞 stood 之前。

例2 A girl stood on the street corner.

→ On the street corner stood a girl.
有個女孩站在街角。

💡Tips a girl 為名詞,搭配口訣可知倒裝的順序應為:地方副詞 + 動 + 名,所以名詞 a girl 要放在動詞 stood 之後。

例3 A post office is located on top of the hill.

→ On top of the hill is located a post office.

山丘頂上有家郵局。

例4 They talked happily in the backyard.

→ In the backyard they talked happily.

他們在院子裡談得很愉快。

✎ 練功坊

翻譯題

1. Tom 的爸爸正在書房閱讀。(請以地方副詞為句首)

_____

2. 他坐在椅子上。(請以地方副詞為句首)

_____

76
$$\begin{cases} S + V + only\ if + S + V \\ Only\ if + S + V + aux. + S + V \end{cases}$$ 只有…

$$\begin{cases} S + V + only\ when + S + V \\ Only\ when + S + V + aux. + S + V \end{cases}$$ 只有當…

說明▶

Only 在句首時，後面的主要子句須倒裝。Only if 和 Only when 兩者的句意差不多，前者意思是「只有…」；後者意思是「只有當…」。

例1 Daniel's mom will take him to the movies only if he behaves himself.

→ Only if Daniel behaves himself will his mom take him to the movies.

只有 Daniel 守規矩，他媽媽才會帶他去看電影。

例2 The Lunar New Year means a lot only when family members get together.

→ Only when family members get together does the Lunar New Year mean a lot.

只有在家人團聚時，春節才會有意義。

例3 Only when we are well prepared can we do things well.
只有當我們準備充分，我們才能把事情做好。

例4 Only if you love yourself will you be loved.
只有你愛自己，別人才會愛你。

句型比較

S + V + only + to V　…卻…

說明 此句型表示「卻…」，only 不在句首，所以不須倒裝。

例1 He rang the doorbell many times only to find that nobody was home.
他按門鈴好幾次，卻發現沒人在家。

例2 We hurried to the airport only to find that we left the passports and plane tickets at home.
我們趕到機場，卻發現把護照和機票忘在家裡。

練功坊

翻譯題

1. Bill 只有在有考試時才會讀書。

_____

2. Andy 只有在心情好時才會提供幫助。

_____

3. Steve 衝到餐廳卻發現它打烊了。

_____

77 What + (a/an) + adj. + N (+ S + V)!　　…多麼…啊！
How + adj. (+ S + V)!

說明

此句型為感嘆句用法，what 後須接名詞，how 後接形容詞。如果不寫出句子最後的主詞及動詞也不影響句意的話，則句子最後的主詞及動詞可省略。

例1 What a huge toy (it is)!

　　→ How huge the toy is!

多麼巨大的玩具啊！

Tips What a huge toy! 的句意和 What a huge toy it is! 的句意一樣清楚，故句尾的 it is 可省略。

例2 What diligent workers (they are)!

　　→ How diligent the workers are!

多麼勤奮的工人啊！

例3 What a wonderful invention the cellphone is!

手機是多麼棒的發明啊！

例4 How wonderful the cellphone is!

這手機好棒啊！

例5 What a humorous teacher David is!

David 是多麼幽默的老師啊！

例6 How humorous David is!

David 真是幽默啊！

練功坊

翻譯題

1. 多麼英勇的士兵啊！

　　_____

2. 多麼頑皮的一個男孩啊！

　　_____

78 It is/was + N + that...　就是…，正是…

說明

此一句型為強調句，把要強調的部分放在 it is/was 和 that 中間即可。

〔例1〕 It was Nancy that met Eason in the park yesterday.
昨天在公園裡遇到 Eason 的正是 Nancy。

　Tips 此句強調 Nancy。

〔例2〕 It was yesterday that Nancy met Eason in the park.
就是昨天 Nancy 在公園裡遇到 Eason。

　Tips 此句強調 yesterday。

〔例3〕 It was in the park that Nancy met Eason yesterday.
Nancy 昨天就是在公園裡遇到 Eason。

　Tips 此句強調 in the park。

〔例4〕 It was her financial security that I was worried about.
我所擔心的就是她的財務安全。

〔例5〕 It was the event that united us together.
就是這場盛事讓我們團結在一起。

練功坊

翻譯題

1. 贏得冠軍的正是楊先生。

_____

2. 就是這些飛彈威脅世界安全。

_____

3. 正是 Tom 未能分辨好與壞。

_____

79

S + aux. + not + V...until...

Not until... + aux. + S + V...　　　直到…才…

It is/was not until... + that + S + V...

說明

此句型的意思為「直到…才…」，書寫時須注意句中主詞和動詞位置的變化。

例1 Thomas did not finish his project until yesterday.

   → Not until yesterday did Thomas finish his project.

   → It was not until yesterday that Thomas finished his project.

Thomas 直到昨天才完成他的企劃案。

💭 **Tips** 否定詞 not until 放於句首時，須用倒裝。

例2 I did not know Meryl Streep is such a great actress until I watched the film.

   → Not until I watched the film did I know Meryl Streep is such a great actress.

   → It was not until I watched the film that I knew Meryl Streep is such a great actress.

我直到看了這部電影，才知道梅莉・史翠普是那麼優秀的女演員。

✎ 練功坊

翻譯題

1. 人們直到失去健康，才意識到它的重要性。

2. 他直到來到臺灣，才知道有那麼多便利商店。

80 分數的寫法

    1/3: one-third

    2/5: two-fifths

    137/217: one hundred and thirty seven over two hundred and seventeen

說明

1. 分子用基數 (如 one、two)，分母用序數 (如 first、second)。例如：

• 1/5: one-fifth

• 1/4: one-fourth

💭 **Tips** 1/4 也可以寫成 one quarter。

2. 但須注意 1/2 的寫法為例外，要寫成 one half，不可寫成 one-second。

3. 分子大於 1 時，分母的序數字尾要加上 s。例如：

- 2/3: two-thirds
- 3/7: three-sevenths

4. 數字太大，例如超過一百時，中間的 / 用 over 表示。例如：

- 317/533: three hundred and seventeen over five hundred and thirty three

延伸補充▶

另外也可用 ...out of... 來表達幾分之幾。

例1 Two out of ten students at this school were from foreign countries.
這所學校裡的學生每十個就有兩個來自外國。

例2 Nine out of one thousand people in this country were diagnosed with a rare disease.
這個國家的人民當中，每一千個就有九個被診斷出一種罕見疾病。

✎ 練功坊

請用英文寫出下列分數：

1. 4/5 _____

2. 2/9 _____

3. 7/13 _____

4. 127/319 _____

Chapter 1
動詞相關句型

單元 1

翻譯題

1. Maple leaves turn red in fall.
2. The model looks so beautiful.
3. The food tasted like beef.
4. Alex appeared nervous when he saw the police officer.
5. Milk turns sour soon if it is not put in the fridge.

單元 2

翻譯題

1. I saw Rick surrounded by a lot of fans yesterday.
2. I felt the house shaking when the earthquake occurred.
3. I had my computer fixed last week.

單元 3

翻譯題

1. History is so important that it should not be left forgotten.
2. Rick found a boy crying in the street helplessly.
3. It is everyone's business to keep the environment clean.

單元 4

翻譯題

1. It took Grace four hours to run the marathon.
   → Grace took four hours to run the marathon.
   → Grace spent four hours running the marathon.
2. Jimmy spent NT$8,000 buying the new cellphone/on the new cellphone.

→ The new cellphone cost Jimmy NT$8,000.
→ It cost Jimmy NT$8,000 to buy the new cellphone.

單元 5

翻譯題

1. Since Andy failed math, he could not help but go to a make-up class.
   → Since Andy failed math, he could not help going to a make-up class.
   → Since Andy failed math, he had no choice but to go to a make-up class.
2. Allen could not help but save money on food and other daily expenses in times of economic difficulties.
   → Allen could not help saving money on food and other daily expenses in times of economic difficulties.
   → Allen had no choice but to save money on food and other daily expenses in times of economic difficulties.
3. As soon as Sandy heard the joke, she could not help but laugh.
   → As soon as Sandy heard the joke, she could not help laughing.
   → As soon as Sandy heard the joke, she had no choice but to laugh.

單元 6

翻譯題

1. I used to go jogging three times a week.
2. A lot of foreigners are not used to the humid weather in Taiwan.
3. Knives and forks are used for cutting food.
   → Knives and forks are used to cut food.
4. Laws are used for the protection of people's rights.
   → Laws are used to protect people's rights.

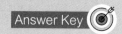

單元 7

翻譯題

1. Jimmy would rather have hot pot at home than eat at a restaurant.
   → Jimmy preferred having hot pot at home to eating at a restaurant.
   → Jimmy preferred to have hot pot at home rather than eat at a restaurant.
2. Grace would rather learn tennis than practice yoga.
   → Grace preferred learning tennis to practicing yoga.
   → Grace preferred to learn tennis rather than practice yoga.

單元 8

翻譯題

1. Parents usually see/view playing online games as a waste of time.
   → Parents usually regard/take/perceive playing online games as a waste of time.
   → Parents usually think of/look (up)on playing online games as a waste of time.
2. The subject is seen/viewed as very important.
   → The subject is regarded/taken/perceived as very important.
   → The subject is thought of/looked (up)on as very important.

單元 9

翻譯題

1. Dave was accused of murder.
2. The man robbed Betty of her expensive bag.
3. The photo reminded Rick of his beloved grandma.

單元 10

翻譯題

1. The organization comprises the United States, Canada, and 27 European countries.
   → The organization consists of the United States, Canada, and 27 European countries.
   → The organization is comprised/composed of the United States, Canada, and 27 European countries.
   → The organization is made up of the United States, Canada, and 27 European countries.
2. The staff comprised Italians and Americans.
   → The staff consisted of Italians and Americans.
   → The staff was comprised/composed of Italians and Americans.
   → The staff was made up of Italians and Americans.

單元 11

翻譯題

1. This museum is located/situated in Chiayi.
   → This museum stands/sits/lies in Chiayi.
2. Kenting National Park is located/situated in the southern part of Taiwan.
   → Kenting National Park stands/sits/lies in the southern part of Taiwan.
3. My house is located/situated in a small fishing village in eastern Taiwan.
   → My house stands/sits/lies in a small fishing village in eastern Taiwan.

單元 12

翻譯題

1. Something lucky happened to Alex yesterday, so he was pleased.
2. A tornado occurred and destroyed 40 houses in the small town.
3. The bag belongs to the little girl with long hair.
4. Our school anniversary celebration takes place in November every year.

Chapter 2
助動詞相關句型

單元 13

翻譯題

1. Tom has been in Japan since last summer.
2. Cellphones have been widely used in recent years.
3. Helen has not been to the U.S. so far.

單元 14

翻譯題

1. By the time David completes/finishes the book, he will have written three books.
2. By the time Steve and Nancy got married, they had dated for ten years.
3. By the time school starts in September, I will have become a senior.

單元 15

翻譯題

1. My wallet must be put in the drawer.
2. Peter must have got/gotten drunk last night.
3. I should have handed in/turned in/submitted the report last week.
4. They could/might/may have formed/established/set up a new company.

單元 16

翻譯題

1. The emperor ordered that Valentine be put to death.
2. Father advised that I go back home before 11 p.m.
3. The company required that every employee wear the uniform.

單元 17

翻譯題

1. Daniel left home earlier this morning for fear of traffic jams.
   → Daniel left home earlier this morning for fear that there might be traffic jams.
   → Daniel left home earlier this morning lest there (should) be traffic jams.
2. Grace told Tim a white lie for fear of hurting his feelings.
   → Grace told Tim a white lie for fear that she might hurt his feelings.
   → Grace told Tim a white lie lest she (should) hurt his feelings.

Chapter 3
動狀詞相關句型

單元 18

翻譯題

1. To/In order to work efficiently, you need good time management.
   → You need good time management in order to/so as to/to work efficiently.
   → You need good time management with a view to/with an eye to working efficiently.
   → You need good time management in order that/so that you can work efficiently.
2. To/In order to celebrate the New Year, American families get together at the end of December.
   → American families get together at the end of December in order to/so as to/to celebrate the New Year.
   → American families get together at the end of December with an eye to/with a view to celebrating the New Year.
   → American families get together at the end of December in order that/so that they can

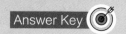

celebrate the New Year.

單元 19

選擇題

1. C 2. A 3. C 4. B

單元 20

翻譯題

1. People have trouble/difficulty/a hard time/problems living well without the help of others.
   → It is difficult for people to live well without the help of others.
2. Ordinary people have trouble/difficulty/a hard time/problems running a marathon without proper training.
   → It is difficult for ordinary people to run a marathon without proper training.
3. Can you imagine living in outer space?

單元 21

翻譯題

1. There is no predicting when the typhoon will hit the small island.
2. There is no parking in this area.
3. There are some people protesting against injustice of housing.
4. There are some children not able to go to school in remote villages.

單元 22

翻譯題

1. Bought from the supermarket, the seafood was very fresh.
2. Finding no people around, the thief broke into the house.

單元 23

翻譯題

1. My father is sitting on the chair with his legs crossed.
2. Mary did not answer, with her head shaking.
3. The old woman did not say anything, with tears rolling down her face.

單元 24

翻譯題

1. Thirty people got killed in the car accident, including the driver and the tour guide.
   → Thirty people got killed in the car accident, the driver and the tour guide included.
   → Thirty people got killed in the car accident, inclusive of the driver and the tour guide.
2. Seven people won the lottery, including David and his son.
   → Seven people won the lottery, David and his son included.
   → Seven people won the lottery, inclusive of David and his son.

Chapter 4
代名詞相關句型

單元 25

選擇題

1. C 2. A 3. B 4. A 5. C

單元 26

翻譯題

1. Someone special is visiting our school next Wednesday.
2. I really don't want to say anything bad about him.
3. Nothing awful happened yesterday.

單元 27

翻譯題

1. The fire had a lot to do with Rick's neglect.
2. The city's prosperity has something to do with its mayor.
3. Alex's excellent performance had a little to do with his personality.

Chapter 5
形容詞與副詞相關句型

單元 28

翻譯題

1. Following the traffic rules when you drive is important.
   → Following the traffic rules when you drive is of great importance.
2. I really do not own anything valuable.
   → I really do not own anything of great value.

單元 29

翻譯題

1. (Much) to the regret of him, he didn't attend his daughter's graduation ceremony.
   → (Much) to his regret, he didn't attend his daughter's graduation ceremony.
2. (Much) to the surprise of me, he broke up with Tina last week.
   → (Much) to my surprise, he broke up with Tina last week.
3. (Much) to the delight of Darren and his younger brother, his father bought a new house.
   → (Much) to Darren and his younger brother's delight, his father bought a new house.
4. (Much) to the delight of her, the class reunion is an unexpected success.
   → (Much) to her delight, the class reunion is an unexpected success.

單元 30

翻譯題

1. Mt. Jade (Yushan) is a lot/much/far higher than Mt. Ali (Alishan).
2. Taking the MRT is slightly/a little/a bit more expensive than riding a public bike.
3. Riding a motorcycle in Taiwan is even/still more popular than in America.
4. Linda is very grateful to her parents for their help.

單元 31

翻譯題

1. The more you exercise, the healthier you get.
2. The more healthily I eat, the better I feel.
3. The happier you are, the longer you live.
4. The less you want, the more satisfied you are.

單元 32

翻譯題

1. The building is six times as high as that one.
   → The building is six times higher than that one.
   → The building is six times the height of that one.
2. The sports car is four times as expensive as that one.
   → The sports car is four times more expensive than that one.
   → The sports car is four times the cost of that one.
3. My land is five times as large as yours.
   → My land is five times larger than yours.
   → My land is five times the size of yours.

單元 33

翻譯題

1. She works as hard as her sister (does).
2. The supermarket does not make so/as much

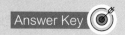

noise as the night market (does).

→ The supermarket is not so/as noisy as the night market.

3. Fred drank as much water as Alex (did).

單元 34

翻譯題

1. Jane promised to return the book as soon as possible.

→ Jane promised to return the book as soon as she could.

2. Brad tried to listen as carefully as possible.

→ Brad tried to listen as carefully as he could.

3. I will do the job as well as possible.

→ I will do the job as well as I can.

Chapter 6
介系詞相關句型

單元 35

翻譯題

1. Tom was opposed to doing what his parents told him to do.

→ Tom objected to doing what his parents told him to do.

2. He is looking forward to seeing his good friend(s) again.

3. He devoted himself to improving the quality of life in his community.

單元 36

翻譯題

1. Doing a warm-up before exercise can prevent you from getting hurt.

2. Bad weather stopped us from taking a trip to Hualien.

3. A sudden accident deterred the couple from arriving at the wedding on time.

單元 37

填空題

1. for   2. as

翻譯題

3. Taiwan is famous/noted/known/well-known/renowned for making advanced computers.

4. Mark is famous/noted/known/well-known/renowned for doing voluntary work.

→ Mark is famous/noted/known/well-known/renowned as a voluntary worker.

單元 38

翻譯題

1. Steve was addicted to alcohol and often got drunk.

2. Mark indulged in online shopping and often bought some unnecessary items.

3. Fred was absorbed/immersed in watching TV and did not notice Rick coming.

→ Fred buried/immersed himself in watching TV and did not notice Rick coming.

單元 39

翻譯題

1. Steve usually takes exercise on weekends instead of/rather than wasting time playing online games.

→ Steve usually takes exercise on weekends rather than waste time playing online games.

→ Instead of/Rather than wasting time playing online games, Steve usually takes exercise on weekends.

→ Rather than waste time playing online games, Steve usually takes exercise on weekends.

→ Steve doesn't waste time playing online games; instead, he usually takes exercise on weekends.

→ Steve doesn't waste time playing online

games. Instead/Rather, he usually takes exercise on weekends.

→ Steve doesn't waste time playing online games; he usually takes exercise on weekends instead.

2. I enjoy having local delicacies at the night market instead of/rather than eating at a restaurant.

→ I enjoy having local delicacies at the night market rather than eat at a restaurant.

→ Instead of/Rather than eating at a restaurant, I enjoy having local delicacies at the night market.

→ Rather than eat at a restaurant, I enjoy having local delicacies at the night market.

→ I don't enjoy eating at a restaurant; instead, I enjoy having local delicacies at the night market.

→ I don't enjoy eating at a restaurant. Instead/Rather, I enjoy having local delicacies at the night market.

→ I don't enjoy eating at a restaurant; I enjoy having local delicacies at the night market instead.

單元 40

翻譯題

1. The typhoon led to/contributed to/gave rise to/resulted in/brought about landslides and floods.

2. The devastating traffic accident led to/contributed to/gave rise to/resulted in/brought about the closure of the roads.

3. The severe drought led to/contributed to/gave rise to/resulted in/brought about food shortage.

Chapter 7
連接詞相關句型

單元 41

翻譯題

1. Nick put his book bag on the desk, and so did Betty.

2. Joseph is a hard-working student, and so is Linda.

3. I don't like spicy food, and neither/nor does my sister.

單元 42

翻譯題

1. You have to pay the tax on time, or you will get fined.

→ You have to pay the tax on time; otherwise, you will get fined.

→ You have to pay the tax on time. Otherwise, you will get fined.

2. Rick needs to get home before 11 p.m., or he will get punished by his mom.

→ Rick needs to get home before 11 p.m.; otherwise, he will get punished by his mom.

→ Rick needs to get home before 11 p.m. Otherwise, he will get punished by his mom.

3. Hurry up, or we might be late.

→ Hurry up; otherwise, we might be late.

→ Hurry up. Otherwise, we might be late.

4. We might be late unless we hurry up.

單元 43

翻譯題

1. Allen neither studies hard nor works hard.

2. Either Sandy or Mary will win the race.

3. We as well as Joe go jogging every morning.

4. Not only Steve but also a lot of other students had fun at the party.

單元 44

翻譯題

1. As soon as/The moment/The instant/The minute I saw Mary, I walked away without saying anything.
   → Upon/On seeing Mary, I walked away without saying anything.
   → No sooner had I seen Mary than I walked away without saying anything.

2. As soon as/The moment/The instant/The minute my brother heard the alarm clock ringing, he jumped out of bed right away.
   → Upon/On hearing the alarm clock ringing, my brother jumped out of bed right away.
   → No sooner had my brother heard the alarm clock ringing than he jumped out of bed right away.

單元 45

翻譯題

1. Brad moved so that/in order that he could be closer to his school.

2. The supermodel is so beautiful and kind that a lot of people like her.
   → She is such a beautiful and kind supermodel that a lot of people like her.

單元 46

翻譯題

1. Whether you will come to my birthday party (or not) doesn't matter.
   → It doesn't matter whether/if you will come to my birthday party (or not).

2. Whether you succeed or fail, I will support you.

3. Whether you help me (or not), I will do the project.

4. I'm not sure whether/if I understand what he means (or not).

單元 47

翻譯題

1. Although/Though he got poor grades, he still studied hard.
   → Despite/In spite of the fact that he got poor grades, he still studied hard.
   → Despite/In spite of/Notwithstanding getting poor grades, he still studied hard.

2. Although/Though Harry Brown is a millionaire, he still works hard.
   → Despite/In spite of the fact that Harry Brown is a millionaire, he still works hard.
   → Despite/In spite of/Notwithstanding being a millionaire, Harry Brown still works hard.

單元 48

翻譯題

1. (As) carefully as Ted listened, he still couldn't understand what the teacher said.
   → Although Ted listened carefully, he still couldn't understand what the teacher said.

2. (As) slowly as the old man walked, he still climbed to the top of the mountain.
   → Although the old man walked slowly, he still climbed to the top of the mountain.

3. (As) repeatedly as May failed, she still didn't give up.
   → Although May failed repeatedly, she still didn't give up.

單元 49

翻譯題

1. Mark was fishing while I was jogging by the lake.
   → While I was jogging by the lake, Mark was fishing.

2. My mom likes shopping while my dad likes staying at home.

3. While it was raining, we still decided to go on a picnic.

→ Although/Though it was raining, we still decided to go on a picnic.

→ I saw a lot of marathon runners, and some of them came from Kenya.

單元 50

翻譯題

1. Joe failed English and math because of/as a result of/owing to/due to his laziness.
2. I quit the job because I have not got paid for three months.
3. Thanks to his understanding, I felt a sigh of relief.

單元 51

選擇題

1. D   2. AB

翻譯題

3. Because/Since it was raining, traffic got worse.
   → Traffic got worse because/since it was raining.
   → Traffic got worse, for it was raining.
4. Because/Since there was no audience, the performers felt discouraged.
   → The performers felt discouraged because/since there was no audience.
   → The performers felt discouraged, for there was no audience.

Chapter 8
關係代名詞、副詞與名詞子句相關句型

單元 52

選擇題

1. C   2. C   3. A   4. A

翻譯題

5. I saw a lot of marathon runners, some of whom came from Kenya.

單元 53

翻譯題

1. What/All (that) Kevin has to do is (to) go on a diet and keep exercising.
2. What/All (that) the mayor needs to do is (to) make the city government work better.
3. What/All (that) my father has to do at home every day is (to) clean the house and cook dinner.

單元 54

翻譯題

1. Whoever knew Rick knew that he was from the small country in South America.
2. I don't like whoever is always late.
3. Among the four books, you may take whichever you like.

單元 55

翻譯題

1. *Star Wars* is the best movie that I have ever seen.
2. The most expensive bike that Jason had ever bought was NT$25,000.

單元 56

翻譯題

1. The fact that he is an American surprised me.
2. I am happy about the fact that my grandma got well.
3. The idea that globalization causes more problems seems to be true.

單元 57

翻譯題

1. I don't believe what Helen has said.

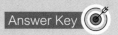

2. How Alex met his girlfriend really interested me.
→ I was really interested in how Alex met his girlfriend.
3. You are what you eat.

Chapter 9
虛主詞與虛受詞相關句型

單元 58

翻譯題

1. It occurred to me this morning that I didn't have school today.
→ It struck me this morning that I didn't have school today.
→ It dawned on me this morning that I didn't have school today.
2. It occurred to Tim that he needed to take his mom to see a doctor.
→ It struck Tim that he needed to take his mom to see a doctor.
→ It dawned on Tim that he needed to take his mom to see a doctor.
3. It occurred to Fred that he hadn't seen his cousin for two years.
→ It struck Fred that he hadn't seen his cousin for two years.
→ It dawned on Fred that he hadn't seen his cousin for two years.

單元 59

翻譯題

1. It was not surprising that my brother, a(n) lazy/idle student, did not pass the exam.
→ It came as no surprise that my brother, a(n) lazy/idle student, did not pass the exam.
→ Unsurprisingly, my brother, a(n) lazy/idle student, did not pass the exam.
2. It was not surprising that Johnny, both tall and handsome, became a supermodel.

→ It came as no surprise that Johnny, both tall and handsome, became a supermodel.
→ Unsurprisingly, Johnny, both tall and handsome, became a supermodel.

單元 60

翻譯題

1. It is likely that Josh will move to Tainan next month.
→ Josh is likely to move to Tainan next month.
2. It is likely that Sarah will go mountain climbing this weekend.
→ Sarah is likely to go mountain climbing this weekend.
3. It is likely that Lily will buy a new house next year.
→ Lily is likely to buy a new house next year.

單元 61

翻譯題

1. It is important/vital/crucial/critical/necessary/essential that drivers (should) pay attention to traffic signs when driving.
2. It is important/vital/crucial/critical/necessary/essential that people (should) protect the environment.
3. It is important/vital/crucial/critical/necessary/essential that you (should) control your weight.
4. It is important/vital/crucial/critical/necessary/essential that students (should) go to school on time.

單元 62

翻譯題

1. Alex seems to be a good tennis player.
→ It seems that Alex is a good tennis player.
2. It seemed that Daniel made a big mistake.
→ Daniel seemed to have made a big mistake.
3. They seem to have worked together for a long time.

→ It seems that they have worked together for a long time.

單元 63

翻譯題

1. It is easy for you to run 5 km(s)/5 kilometers in 30 minutes.
   → To run 5 km(s)/5 kilometers in 30 minutes is easy for you.
   → Running 5 km(s)/5 kilometers in 30 minutes is easy for you.
2. Allen is too shy to speak in public.
3. It is too late for Bob to apologize.

單元 64

翻譯題

1. Rumor has it that Mary cheated on her husband.
2. It is said that the minister will resign soon.
   → People/They say that the minister will resign soon.
3. Legend has it that there is a couple living in the cave.

單元 65

翻譯題

1. The loud noise outside made it hard for students to be attentive in class.
2. Andy found it tiring to work part-time three times a week.
3. Helen considered it worthy to spend time mastering a foreign language.

Chapter 10
假設用法相關句型

單元 66

翻譯題

1. If I exercised more every day, I would become more energetic.
2. If Tom had studied harder last year, he could have got into a better college.
   → Had Tom studied harder last year, he could have got into a better college.

單元 67

翻譯題

1. If it were not for my advice, Daniel might make the mistake again.
   → Were it not for my advice, Daniel might make the mistake again.
2. If it had not been for my teacher's suggestion then, I might have majored in math.
   → Had it not been for my teacher's suggestion then, I might have majored in math.
3. If it had not been for the successful surgery last year, Alex might have died.
   → Had it not been for the successful surgery last year, Alex might have died.

單元 68

翻譯題

1. I wish (that) I could have bought a new car last year.
2. I wish (that) I had enough free time to do what I want to do.
3. I wish my parents good health.

單元 69

翻譯題

1. It's (high) time for Tom to tell the truth.
   → It's (high) time that Tom told the truth.
2. It's (high) time for the president to make the right choice.
   → It's (high) time that the president made the right choice.
3. It's (high) time for us to turn in the assignments.
   → It's (high) time that we turned in the

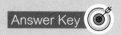

assignments.

Chapter 11
否定用法相關句型

單元 70

翻譯題

1. Joe never comes to Tainan without paying a visit to me.
2. There is no happiness without health.
3. The trip would not be complete without visiting Disneyland.

單元 71

翻譯題

1. It can't be denied that diligence is the key to success.
   → There is no denying that diligence is the key to success.
   → No one can deny that diligence is the key to success.
2. It can't be denied that health is more important than anything else.
   → There is no denying that health is more important than anything else.
   → No one can deny that health is more important than anything else.
3. It can't be denied that education is a very powerful weapon.
   → There is no denying that education is a very powerful weapon.
   → No one can deny that education is a very powerful weapon.

單元 72

翻譯題

1. Parents cannot/can't/can never be too careful in taking care of their children.

→ Parents cannot/can't/can never be careful enough in taking care of their children.
2. You cannot/can't/can never check your account too carefully when withdrawing money.
   → You cannot/can't/can never check your account carefully enough when withdrawing money.

單元 73

翻譯題

1. Jane can ride a motorbike, not to mention/not to speak of/to say nothing of a bike.
2. The old man could not walk, not to mention/not to speak of/to say nothing of running.
   → The old man could not walk, let alone/much less run.
3. The woman could not lift the small box, not to mention/not to speak of/to say nothing of the big desk.
   → The woman could not lift the small box, let alone/much less the big desk.

Chapter 12
特殊句構相關句型

單元 74

翻譯題

1. Seldom does she eat porridge or rice for breakfast.
2. Hardly/Rarely does Alex have time to rest because he is too busy.

單元 75

翻譯題

1. In the study is Tom's father reading.
2. On the chair he sat.

單元 76

翻譯題

1. Bill studies only if there is a test.
   → Only if there is a test does Bill study.

2. Andy offers help only when he is in a good mood.
   → Only when Andy is in a good mood does he offer help.

3. Steve rushed to the restaurant only to find that it was closed.

單元 77

翻譯題

1. What brave soldiers (they are)!
   → How brave the soldiers are!

2. What a naughty boy (he is)!
   → How naughty the boy is!

單元 78

翻譯題

1. It was Mr. Yang that won the championship.

2. It was the missiles that threatened world security.

3. It was Tom that failed to distinguish between good and bad.

單元 79

翻譯題

1. People do not realize the importance of health until they lose it.
   → Not until people lose their health do they realize its importance.
   → It is not until people lose their health that they realize its importance.

2. He did not know there are so many convenience stores until he came to Taiwan.
   → Not until he came to Taiwan did he know there are so many convenience stores.
   → It was not until he came to Taiwan that he knew there are so many convenience stores.

單元 80

1. four-fifths
2. two-ninths
3. seven-thirteenths
4. one hundred and twenty seven over three hundred and nineteen

本書圖片來源：Shutterstock

英文學測奪標：考前衝刺100天

王靖賢、林詠梅、張瑛珆、劉家慧／編著

★超詳盡應考策略：
針對學測六大題型，從準備考試的複習方式，到實際應考的答題技巧，應有盡有！

★超精選單字片語：
收錄學測必備單字1,000及片語200，並補充生字、介系詞及重點句型，讓你一書在手，完美複習！

★超豐富模擬試題：
20回考前模擬試題，題題切中核心，打通英文任督二脈，保證讓你越寫越有自信，大考高分So Easy！

★超完美作文解析：
含10篇歷屆學測試題的作文練習，附有優秀範文與詳實解析，讓你溫故知新，百戰百勝！

英文指考致勝：考前衝刺100天

王靖賢、曲成彬、周彩蓉、蘇文賢／編著

★超詳盡應考策略：
針對指考七大題型，從準備考試的複習方式，到實際應考的答題技巧，應有盡有！

★超精選單字片語：
收錄指考必備單字1,000及片語200，並補充生字、介系詞及重點句型，讓你一書在手，完美複習！

★超豐富模擬試題：
20回考前模擬試題，題題切中核心，打通英文任督二脈，保證讓你越寫越有自信，大考高分So Easy！

★超完美作文解析：
含10篇歷屆指考試題的作文練習，附有優秀範文與詳實解析，讓你溫故知新，百戰百勝！

新多益黃金互動16週：
基礎篇／進階篇

李海碩、張秀帆、多益900團隊／編著
Joseph E. Schier／審訂

依難易度分為基礎篇與進階篇，方便依程度選用。

★ 本書由 ETS 認證多益英語測驗專業發展工作坊講師李海碩、張秀帆編寫，及多益模擬試題編寫者 Joseph E. Schier 審訂。

★ 涵蓋 2018 年 3 月最新改制多益題型。兩冊各 8 單元，皆附聽力光碟及一份多益全真模擬試題。

英語 *Make Me High* 系列

學測指考英文 致勝句型

隨堂評量

王隆興　編著

掌握關鍵，瞄準致勝！

關鍵 *1* 名師嚴選80個句型重點！
完整收錄大考常見句型，並比較易混淆的句型，清楚掌握重點，舉一反三。

關鍵 *2* 解說清楚明瞭一看就懂！
重點一目瞭然，說明淺顯易懂好吸收，考前衝刺神隊友，迅速提升考場即戰力。

關鍵 *3* 隨堂評量實戰練習現學現用！
隨書附贈20回隨堂評量，及時檢視學習成果、熟悉句型，以收事半功倍之效。

學測指考英文致勝句型**隨堂評量** Table of Contents

第 1 回	Chapter 1	動詞相關句型 (單元 1～4)	01
第 2 回	Chapter 1	動詞相關句型 (單元 5～8)	03
第 3 回	Chapter 1	動詞相關句型 (單元 9～12)	05
第 4 回	Chapter 2	助動詞相關句型 (單元 13～17)	07
第 5 回	Chapter 3	動狀詞相關句型 (單元 18～20)	09
第 6 回	Chapter 3	動狀詞相關句型 (單元 21～24)	11
第 7 回	Chapter 4	代名詞相關句型 (單元 25～27)	13
第 8 回	Chapter 5	形容詞與副詞相關句型 (單元 28～30)	15
第 9 回	Chapter 5	形容詞與副詞相關句型 (單元 31～34)	17
第 10 回	Chapter 6	介系詞相關句型 (單元 35～40)	19
第 11 回	Chapter 7	連接詞相關句型 (單元 41～44)	21
第 12 回	Chapter 7	連接詞相關句型 (單元 45～48)	23
第 13 回	Chapter 7	連接詞相關句型 (單元 49～51)	25
第 14 回	Chapter 8	關係代名詞、副詞與名詞子句相關句型 (單元 52～57)	27
第 15 回	Chapter 9	虛主詞與虛受詞相關句型 (單元 58～61)	29
第 16 回	Chapter 9	虛主詞與虛受詞相關句型 (單元 62～65)	31
第 17 回	Chapter 10	假設用法相關句型 (單元 66～69)	33
第 18 回	Chapter 11	否定用法相關句型 (單元 70～73)	35
第 19 回	Chapter 12	特殊句構相關句型 (單元 74～77)	37
第 20 回	Chapter 12	特殊句構相關句型 (單元 78～80)	39

Answer Key 41

I. 選擇題 (每題 5%)

(   ) 1. Tom looked _____ at his son.

     (A) angry   (B) anger   (C) angrily   (D) angering

(   ) 2. How does the new watch _____ ?

     (A) look   (B) look like   (C) looked   (D) be looking

(   ) 3. I saw the window _____ by Steve.

     (A) to break   (B) break   (C) breaking   (D) broken

(   ) 4. Mary found her brother _____ basketball yesterday.

     (A) play   (B) playing   (C) to play   (D) plays

(   ) 5. My mom _____ NT$2,500 buying a new bike.

     (A) spent   (B) took   (C) cost   (D) bought

II. 填充題：請填入適當的詞或詞性變化，每格一字 (每題 5%)

_____ 1. We often keep our doors _____ (close) when sleeping at night.

_____ 2. Fred seemed _____ (happiness) at the party.

_____ 3. The great book _____ me NT$300.

_____ 4. I didn't see the bike _____ (steal), but it was just gone.

_____ 5. Bob was seen _____ (ride) a bike in the park.

III. 合併與改寫：請用適當的詞來合併與改寫句子 (每題 5%)

1. I bought the watch for NT$1,500. (請用動詞 spend 改寫)

_____

2. How does beef taste? (請用 delicious 作答)

_____

3. I saw Grace in the park. She was running there. (請用 S + V + O + OC 的句型合併)

_____

4. I spend 30 minutes doing my homework every day. (請用動詞 take 改寫)

_____

5. I found Eric in the room. He was crying there. (請用 S + V + O + OC 的句型合併)

_____

IV. 整句式翻譯 (每題 5%)

1. 當遇到麻煩時，Alex 總是保持冷靜。

_____

2. 我聽到 Mary 在隔壁房間和她弟弟聊天。

_____

3. 颱風使得數百人無家可歸。(請用 S + leave + O + OC 的句型作答)

_____

4. 我每天花 50 分鐘看電視新聞。

_____

5. 這本新書花了我 500 元。

_____

I. 選擇題 (每題 5%)

(   ) 1. Andy couldn't help _____ when he found his new cellphone stolen.

     (A) crying   (B) to cry   (C) cry   (D) cried

(   ) 2. David had no choice but _____ in after he had tried his best.

     (A) give   (B) to give   (C) giving   (D) to giving

(   ) 3. Alex is used to _____ in the morning.

     (A) run   (B) running   (C) be running   (D) ran

(   ) 4. Daniel preferred to _____ shopping.

     (A) went   (B) go to   (C) going   (D) go

(   ) 5. Rick _____ it a must to study at least five hours a day.

     (A) viewed   (B) saw   (C) thought of   (D) considered

II. 填充題：請填入適當的詞或詞性變化，每格一字 (每題 5%)

_____ 1. I couldn't help but _____ (sell) my car since I was in need of money.

_____ 2. A key is used to _____ (open) the door.

_____ 3. Mary used to _____ (go) to cram school without eating dinner.

_____ 4. Sandy preferred to have salad for breakfast rather than just _____ (drink) a cup of coffee.

_____ 5. The teacher regarded him _____ the smartest student in the class.

III. 合併與改寫：請用適當的詞來合併與改寫句子 (每題 5%)

1. Sarah had no choice but to buy her brother a new computer. (請用 could not help... 改寫)

_____

2. Brad often played tennis in the evening. (請用 used to... 改寫)

_____

3. I like tea better than coffee. (請用 prefer...to... 改寫)

_____

4. Nancy would rather watch TV at home than go window-shopping. (請用 prefer to... 改寫)

_____

5. I think that Mary is a hard-working person. (請用 regard... 改寫)

_____

IV. 整句式翻譯 (每題 5%)

1. 很多人認為 Will 是一位好投手。

_____

2. Nancy 寧願走路也不願開車。

_____

3. Allen 以前常吃米飯當早餐。

_____

4. George 不適應臺北繁忙的交通。

_____

5. Rick 看見這位孤單老人時，忍不住哭了出來。

_____

I. 選擇題 (每題 5%)

( ) 1. Joe was accused _____ stealing Henry's new bike.

    (A) with   (B) of   (C) to   (D) in

( ) 2. The research team _____ ten professors.

    (A) comprised   (B) was comprised   (C) composed of   (D) consisted

( ) 3. The bookstore _____ on the street corner.

    (A) is stood   (B) locates   (C) is located   (D) situates

( ) 4. The new house _____ Johnny.

    (A) was belonged   (B) was belonged to

    (C) belonged to   (D) has belonged

( ) 5. A car accident _____ Erick last weekend.

    (A) was happened   (B) was happened to

    (C) happened to   (D) took place to

II. 填充題：請填入適當的詞或詞性變化，每格一字 (每題 5%)

_____ 1. The picture reminded me _____ my grandfather.

_____ 2. The club is made up _____ 1,500 members.

_____ 3. Our school stands on Main Street. = Our school is _____ on Main Street.

_____ 4. An earthquake _____ in Sri Lanka and killed many people.

_____ 5. I happened _____ meet my long-lost friend on the street yesterday.

III. 合併與改寫：請用適當的詞來合併與改寫句子 (每題 5%)

1. We told Tom the good news. (請用動詞 inform 改寫)

   _____

2. The basketball team is composed of ten players. (請用動詞 consist 改寫)

   _____

3. The post office lies behind the tall building. (請用動詞 situate 改寫)

   _____

4. Miss Lin owns the diamond ring. (請用動詞 belong to 改寫)

   _____

5. A big celebration is held every year to honor the war heroes. (請用動詞 take place 改寫)

   _____

IV. 整句式翻譯 (每題 5%)

1. Richard 被剝奪投票的權利。

   _____

2. 搶匪搶了 Amy 的項鍊。

   _____

3. 我們班是由 20 個學生所組成。

   _____

4. 這家餐廳位於繁忙的街上。

   _____

5. 這間學校的校慶於每年 11 月舉行。

   _____

I. 選擇題 (每題 5%)

(   ) 1. Andrew _____ in Taipei since he was born.

       (A) is living   (B) lives   (C) has living   (D) has lived

(   ) 2. By the time my father comes home, I _____.

       (A) will go to bed   (B) have to go to bed

       (C) will have gone to bed   (D) will have to go to bed

(   ) 3. George _____ last night because he drank a lot.

       (A) must drink   (B) should drink

       (C) must have got drunk   (D) must be drinking

(   ) 4. The emperor ordered that the criminal _____ put to death.

       (A) was   (B) be   (C) should   (D) have

(   ) 5. Alex got up early _____ he go to school late.

       (A) lest   (B) for fear of   (C) for fear that   (D) in order that

II. 填充題：請填入適當的詞或詞性變化，每格一字 (每題 5%)

_____ 1. Wendy has known me _____ 20 years.

_____ 2. By the time I graduate from high school, the house will have _____ sold.

_____ 3. Steve should _____ studied hard before the final exam, but he fooled around.

_____ 4. I suggested that Johnny _____ (take) part in the English speech contest.

_____ 5. Jimmy studied hard lest he _____ (fail) math.

III. 合併與改寫：請用適當的詞來合併與改寫句子 (每題 5%)

1. I was busy yesterday, and I am still busy today. (請用 since yesterday 改寫)

   _____

2. The train had left before I arrived at the station. (請用 By the time... 改寫)

   _____

3. Daniel had to get up early this morning, but he failed to do so. (請用 should have + p.p. 改寫)

   _____

4. Ann insisted on something. Her son had to go to bed before 10 p.m. (請用 Ann insisted that... 改寫)

   _____

5. Fred behaved himself in order not to be punished. (請用 for fear of... 改寫)

   _____

IV. 整句式翻譯 (每題 5%)

1. 最近幾年，智慧型手機一直很流行。

   _____

2. 我到家的時候，媽媽已經離開了。

   _____

3. 我的皮夾一定是在我書包裡。(請用 must 作答)

   _____

4. 老師建議 Miranda 申請研究所 (graduate school)。

   _____

5. Jenny 搭計程車上班以免遲到。

   _____

I. 選擇題 (每題 5%)

( ) 1. The parents walked quietly _____ wake up their baby.

    (A) so as not to   (B) in order that   (C) with an eye to   (D) so that

( ) 2. _____, or you might be late for school.

    (A) To get up early   (B) Get up early

    (C) Getting up early   (D) To getting up early

( ) 3. The old man had difficulty _____.

    (A) to walk   (B) walked   (C) walking   (D) walk

( ) 4. Steven considered _____ to the movies tonight.

    (A) going   (B) to go   (C) go   (D) went

( ) 5. We should try not to use plastic bags _____ protecting the environment.

    (A) with a view to   (B) so as to   (C) in order that   (D) so that to

II. 填充題：請填入適當的詞或詞性變化，每格一字 (每題 5%)

_____ 1. Allen studies hard in _____ to get into a good college.

_____ 2. _____ (practice) basketball every day takes us a lot of time.

_____ 3. _____ (fail) to hand in the term paper on time, Rick felt upset.

_____ 4. Jane had trouble _____ (communicate) with foreigners.

_____ 5. _____ (exercise) regularly, and you will be healthy.

III. 合併與改寫：請用適當的詞來合併與改寫句子 (每題 5%)

1. David walks to work in order to save money. (請用 ...with an eye to... 改寫)

_____

2. Leo got good grades. It really made him happy. (請用 V-ing... 合併)

_____

3. It was hard for Alex to run a marathon in under four hours. (請用 have difficulty... 改寫)

_____

4. Tens of thousands of people gathered in Times Square to celebrate the New Year.
   (請用 ...so that... 改寫)

_____

5. Dennis was asked a personal question. Dennis felt unhappy. (請用分詞構句合併)

_____

IV. 整句式翻譯 (每題 5%)

1. Andy 為了養家努力工作。

_____

2. Rick 沒在晚上 10 點前到家而被他爸爸責罵。(請用以 Not... 開頭的分詞構句作答)

_____

3. Jeff 很難入睡,所以他決定去看醫生。

_____

4. 你介意借給我你的新書嗎?

_____

5. 早睡早起是個好習慣。

_____

第 6 回

單元 21〜24

I. 選擇題 (每題 5%)

(　　) 1. Twenty students took part in the singing contest, Ronny and Jasmine _____.

    (A) including   (B) included   (C) inclusive of   (D) being including

(　　) 2. Shirley walked back to the train station, with a stranger _____ her.

    (A) follow   (B) following   (C) followed   (D) being followed

(　　) 3. _____ directly from a farmers' market, the vegetables are always fresh.

    (A) Buying   (B) Bought   (C) To buy   (D) Buy

(　　) 4. There is no _____ along the street. Follow the rule, or your car will be towed away.

    (A) knowing   (B) telling   (C) parking   (D) predicting

(　　) 5. _____, Daniel always gets to school on time.

    (A) To get up early   (B) To getting up early

    (C) Getting up early   (D) Get up early

II. 填充題：請填入適當的詞或詞性變化，每格一字 (每題 5%)

_____ 1. Ten people took a trip to South Africa, _____ of (包括) my sister.

_____ 2. Steve stood there doing nothing, with his head _____ (shake) violently.

_____ 3. It _____ (be) a rainy day, we stayed home watching TV.

_____ 4. There are many street foods _____ (sell) in the stall.

_____ 5. _____ (practice) the violin every day, Bill wants to be a musician one day.

III. 合併與改寫：請用適當的詞來合併與改寫句子 (每題 5%)

1. Five people bought the TV set at a lower price. Andy was one of them. (請用 ...including... 合併)

   _____

2. Daniel took a rest on the sofa. He crossed his legs. (請用 ...with + O + OC 的句型合併)

   _____

3. William was scolded by his parents. He was in a bad mood. (請用分詞構句合併)

   _____

4. There are five students who are riding their bikes in the park. (請用 There are...V-ing... 改寫)

   _____

5. James saved the drowning boy. He was praised by the mayor. (請用分詞構句合併)

   _____

IV. 整句式翻譯 (每題 5%)

1. Jacob 推薦了十個候選人，包括 Grace。

   _____

2. Charlotte 陷在車陣中而上班遲到。(請用分詞構句作答)

   _____

3. 有十個學生被挑選參加研究生課程。(請用以 There... 開頭的句型作答)

   _____

4. 不知道該怎麼辦，Mia 一言不發地離開了。(請用分詞構句作答)

   _____

5. Paul 對此消息很震驚，手一直發抖。(請用 ...with + O + OC 的句型作答)

   _____

第 7 回

單元 25～27

I. 選擇題 (每題 5%)

(　　) 1. Low fertility rates have _____ to do with financial pressures.

　　(A) a lot of　　　　(B) many　　　　(C) much　　　　(D) a little of

(　　) 2. Success in all aspects of life has _____ to do with one's personality.

　　(A) a few　　　　(B) few　　　　(C) a lot　　　　(D) lots of

(　　) 3. One of my parents is an engineer; _____ is a fashion designer.

　　(A) another　　　(B) other　　　(C) the other　　　(D) one

(　　) 4. I have three new books. One is about outer space, another is about gardening, and _____ is about nanotechnology.

　　(A) still another　　(B) still one　　(C) still other　　(D) the other

(　　) 5. Please do _____.

　　(A) useful something　　　　　　(B) something useful

　　(C) something using　　　　　　(D) using something

II. 填充題：請填入適當的詞或詞性變化，每格一字 (每題 5%)

_____ 1. Some of the workers of the company are from India, and _____ others are from Indonesia.

_____ 2. Crime rates usually have much to do _____ economic development.

_____ 3. A pen is in one of my hands and a ruler is in the _____.

_____ 4. Some people like watching TV, others enjoy going shopping, and still _____ prefer playing sports.

_____ 5. Do you notice _____ strange (任何異常的事) about Mary?

III. 合併與改寫：請用適當的詞來合併與改寫句子 (每題 5%)

1. The mood really has much to do with the weather. (請用 ...have a lot to do with... 改寫)

   _____

2. Mike's performance did not have anything to do with the job training. (請用 ...have nothing to do with... 改寫)

   _____

3. He only has a purple flower, a red flower, and a yellow flower. (請用 One...another...the other... 改寫)

   _____

4. I only have a black dog and a white dog. (請用 One of...the other... 改寫)

   _____

5. Something is happening. It is surprising. (請用 There is... 合併)

   _____

IV. 整句式翻譯 (每題 5%)

1. Adam 的失敗與運氣不好有關。

   _____

2. Alex 的雙胞胎姊姊一個是醫生，一個是公車司機。

   _____

3. Jenny 的好脾氣與她所受的教育有很大的關係。

   _____

4. 有些人較喜歡麵條，有些人則較喜歡米飯。

   _____

5. 今天有任何特別的事嗎？

   _____

I. 選擇題 (每題 5%)

(　　) 1. The storybook is of great _____ to me.

    (A) interest   (B) interested   (C) interesting   (D) being interest

(　　) 2. _____ his parents' surprise, Christopher got good grades in math.

    (A) With   (B) Of   (C) On   (D) To

(　　) 3. Tina did _____ better on the test than Sarah.

    (A) very   (B) a lot of   (C) much   (D) great

(　　) 4. Book One is _____ than Book Two.

    (A) more easier   (B) much easy

    (C) much more easier   (D) much easier

(　　) 5. Adele is _____ tallest girl in her class.

    (A) very   (B) the much   (C) the very   (D) much

II. 填充題：請填入適當的詞或詞性變化，每格一字 (每題 5%)

_____ 1. Pictures are _____ great importance to memory.

_____ 2. To my _____ (delighted), our team won first place.

_____ 3. Sandra bought a much _____ (cheap) flight ticket than Grace did.

_____ 4. Betty is _____ beautiful than Helen. Everyone thinks Betty is the most beautiful girl here.

_____ 5. Much to my _____ (astonish), George won the lottery last week.

III. 合併與改寫：請用適當的詞來合併與改寫句子 (每題 5%)

1. Mom had nothing valuable. (請用 value 改寫)

_____

2. I was surprised. Dave lost the game. (請用 To... 合併)

_____

3. Evelyn is short. Iris is taller. (請用 ...much...than... 合併)

_____

4. Exercise is important to everyone. (請用 importance 改寫)

_____

5. The teacher was disappointed. His students didn't listen to him. (請用 To... 合併)

_____

IV. 整句式翻譯 (每題 5%)

1. 這個手錶對 David 意義重大。(請用 ...of... 作答)

_____

2. 讓 Gary 後悔的是他高中輟學。

_____

3. Ian 寫信比我們多數人更為仔細。

_____

4. Hugo 比 Jerry 年長許多。

_____

5. 讓我們震驚的是，部長涉及了那起醜聞。

_____

I. 選擇題 (每題 5%)

( ) 1. The higher you climb, the _____ you fall.

    (A) more hardly   (B) more harder   (C) harder   (D) hard

( ) 2. The house is three times _____ that one.

    (A) larger as   (B) large as   (C) as larger as   (D) larger than

( ) 3. The river is four times the length _____ that one.

    (A) of   (B) as   (C) to   (D) than

( ) 4. The beef smells _____ the pork.

    (A) as well as   (B) so well as   (C) as good as   (D) as better as

( ) 5. Larry ran a marathon as fast as he _____.

    (A) can   (B) could   (C) does   (D) was

II. 填充題：請填入適當的詞或詞性變化，每格一字 (每題 5%)

_____ 1. The _____ you know about the world, the more knowledgeable you are.

_____ 2. The ruler is three times _____ (long) than the pen.

_____ 3. Leo has as _____ money as I do.

_____ 4. Rex studies as _____ (hard) as Ted.

_____ 5. Vincent wrote the composition as well as _____ (盡可能).

III. 合併與改寫：請用適當的詞來合併與改寫句子 (每題 5%)

1. If you sleep better, you will become healthier. (請用 The..., the... 改寫)

_____

2. My car is expensive. Your car is three times more expensive. (請用 ...than... 合併)

_____

3. Wayne is 30 years old. Lucy is 30 years old, too. (請用 ...as...as... 合併)

_____

4. Margaret has two cars. Nina has two cars, too. (請用 ...as...as... 合併)

_____

5. Phoebe came home as early as possible. (請用 as...as...could 改寫)

_____

IV. 整句式翻譯 (每題 5%)

1. Hazel 想得越多就感到越焦慮。

_____

2. 你想要的越少，就會越容易滿足。

_____

3. 我的頭髮是你的三倍長。

_____

4. 我有跟你一樣多的筆。

_____

5. Craig 盡可能仔細地擬定他的計畫。

_____

I. 選擇題 (每題 5%)

(   ) 1. Rita got used to _____ in the early morning.

     (A) run   (B) ran   (C) running   (D) being running

(   ) 2. Parents always try their best to protect their children _____ being hurt.

     (A) of   (B) with   (C) from   (D) in

(   ) 3. He is noted _____ playing basketball in a professional team.

     (A) as   (B) for   (C) with   (D) of

(   ) 4. Samantha buries herself _____ books.

     (A) in   (B) of   (C) with   (D) at

(   ) 5. Smoking contributes _____ his lung cancer.

     (A) in   (B) of   (C) to   (D) at

II. 填充題：請填入適當的詞或詞性變化，每格一字 (每題 5%)

_____ 1. A lot of people are opposed _____ the building of a nuclear power plant.

_____ 2. David is well-known _____ a great teacher.

_____ 3. Bob indulged himself _____ daydreams.

_____ 4. Daniel was addicted _____ alcohol. He usually got drunk.

_____ 5. Allen likes reading a novel instead _____ writing one of his own.

III. 合併與改寫：請用適當的詞來合併與改寫句子 (每題 5%)

1. Tom will see his girlfriend soon. He is looking forward to it. (請用 look forward to 合併)

_____

2. Francis is famous as an actor. (請用 acting 改寫)

_____

3. Jennifer was absorbed in studying English. (請用 ...immersed... 改寫)

_____

4. Bob didn't go window-shopping. He stayed home helping his mom clean the house.
(請用 ...instead of... 合併)

_____

5. The heavy rain resulted in flooding. (請用 lead to 改寫)

_____

IV. 整句式翻譯 (每題 5%)

1. Anne 致力於幫助窮人。

_____

2. 我會阻止 Brian 犯相同的錯。

_____

3. 很不幸地，他對毒品上癮。

_____

4. Joe 想去打籃球，而不是在家睡覺。

_____

5. Kevin 以身為優秀的律師聞名。

_____

I. 選擇題 (每題 5%)

( ) 1. Ashley read the newspaper, and so _____ Grace.

    (A) does   (B) did   (C) was   (D) is

( ) 2. John only eats two meals a day, and so _____ Anthony and his brother.

    (A) does   (B) do   (C) did   (D) will

( ) 3. You won't succeed _____ you work hard.

    (A) unless   (B) or   (C) otherwise   (D) if

( ) 4. Birds as well as a group of ants _____ in the trees.

    (A) is living   (B) living   (C) live   (D) lives

( ) 5. _____ seeing the fierce dog, Jack ran away.

    (A) As soon as   (B) On   (C) The instant   (D) The minute

II. 填充題：請填入適當的詞或詞性變化，每格一字 (每題 5%)

_____ 1. Eliza stayed up late last night, and so _____ Jennifer.

_____ 2. Neil never goes to bed before 11 p.m., and _____ does Sarah.

_____ 3. Alex will go abroad for advanced studies next year, and _____ will Thomas.

_____ 4. Either you or Tom _____ (need) to help clean the house today.

_____ 5. My father as well as his friends _____ strolling in the park now.

III. 合併與改寫：請用適當的詞來合併與改寫句子 (每題 5%)

1. Nick doesn't like Korean food. Oscar doesn't like it, either. (請用 ...neither... 合併)

_____

2. Eat healthy and light food. Otherwise, you will get sick easily. (請用 or 合併)

_____

3. Daniel works in the factory. Peter works in the factory, too. (請用 Both 合併)

_____

4. Sean ate a hamburger for breakfast. He also drank a cup of coffee for breakfast.

(請用 not only...but also... 合併)

_____

5. Victor walked into the living room. He turned on the air conditioner right away.

(請用 As soon as... 合併)

_____

IV. 整句式翻譯 (每題 5%)

1. 我不懂法語，Lisa 也不懂。

_____

2. 遵守交通規則，否則你會收到罰單。

_____

3. 除非你完成你的作業，否則你不可以出去玩。

_____

4. Darcy 和 Gilbert 兩個都不是工程師。

_____

5. 我一離開家，就開始下雨。

_____

I. 選擇題 (每題 5%)

( ) 1. Grey came to the party _____ he might have a talk with the host.

   (A) such that 　 (B) in order to 　 (C) so that 　 (D) with that

( ) 2. Jasper was _____ a strong man that he could lift the heavy stone.

   (A) such 　 (B) so 　 (C) so that 　 (D) such that

( ) 3. Clara was _____ famous that everyone wants her autograph.

   (A) such 　 (B) so 　 (C) so that 　 (D) such that

( ) 4. _____, he still works hard every day.

   (A) Rich as Sean is (B) Sean is as rich (C) Sean is rich as (D) Rich is as Sean

( ) 5. _____ it is raining outside, Grace goes running as usual.

   (A) Although 　 　 　 (B) Despite

   (C) Notwithstanding 　 (D) In spite of

II. 填充題：請填入適當的詞 (whether、such、as 或 that)，每格一字 (每題 5%)

_____ 1. I have never seen _____ a wise man as Thomas.

_____ 2. We have no idea _____ Jay will come back to Taiwan or not.

_____ 3. Noisy _____ the activities on the school construction sites were, everyone paid their full attention in class.

_____ 4. The car is so expensive _____ few people can afford it.

_____ 5. Robin is _____ a popular movie star that he has a large number of fans.

III. 合併與改寫：請用適當的詞來合併與改寫句子 (每題 5%)

1. Although the task is difficult, I still want to overcome it. (請改寫為 Difficult...)

_____

2. Although he knew it was dangerous, Steve still dived into the water to save his brother. (請改寫為 In spite of...)

_____

3. Tina put a lot of effort into her work to get a pay rise. (請改寫為 ...so that...)

_____

4. Nancy is so reliable that she has won her customers' confidence. (請改寫為 ...such...)

_____

5. Despite his lack of money, Johnny set up his own company without delay. (請改寫為 Although...)

_____

IV. 整句式翻譯 (每題 5%)

1. Edward 留不留在這裡都無所謂。

_____

2. Katie 參加這場演講比賽是為了贏得獎金 (cash prize)。(請用 ...so that... 的句型作答)

_____

3. Daniel 那麼和善以致於每個人都想和他交朋友。(請用 ...such... 的句型作答)

_____

4. 雖然沒賺很多錢，David 過著快樂的生活。

_____

5. 那隻貓雖然看起來很胖，但牠跑得很快。(請用 Fat... 的句型作答)

_____

I. 選擇題 (每題 5%)

( ) 1. Jimmy was sleeping _____ his mom was cooking in the kitchen.

　　(A) for 　　　　(B) while 　　　(C) because 　　　(D) since

( ) 2. The basketball player can't participate in the final game _____ injury.

　　(A) because 　　(B) while 　　　(C) because of 　　(D) since

( ) 3. Mark got fired _____ he leaked secret documents to the press.

　　(A) thanks to 　　(B) because of 　　(C) while 　　　(D) because

( ) 4. _____ his father's financial support, Lawrence succeeded in his business.

　　(A) Thanks to 　　(B) Because 　　(C) For 　　　(D) While

( ) 5. It's natural that some people favor the ruling party _____ others support the opposition party.

　　(A) because 　　(B) since 　　　(C) while 　　　(D) for

II. 填充題：請填入適當的詞 (of、since、while 或 because)，每格一字 (每題 5%)

_____ 1. _____ Jenny was born in the U.S.A., she can speak Taiwanese very well.

_____ 2. The flight has been canceled because _____ bad weather.

_____ 3. Tina got a $10,000 cash prize _____ she won the championship.

_____ 4. A lot of people became homeless _____ of the devastating typhoon.

_____ 5. We decided to go by taxi _____ it was urgent.

III. 合併與改寫：請用適當的詞來合併與改寫句子 (每題 5%)

1. John got promoted because he worked hard. (請改寫為 ...because of...)

   _____

2. Some people don't like stinky tofu. Some people enjoy it. (請用 ...while... 合併)

   _____

3. It is raining hard outside. We can't play basketball. (請用 ...because... 合併)

   _____

4. Jason didn't get good grades. He still didn't give up and worked hard. (請用 While... 合併)

   _____

5. Johnny was watching a football game. Jimmy was sleeping in his room. (請用 ...while... 合併)

   _____

IV. 整句式翻譯 (每題 5%)

1. 雖然我已經和 Wayne 一起工作 20 年了，我仍不了解他。(請用 While... 作答)

   _____

2. 有些學生喜歡藝術，有些則喜歡自然科學。

   _____

3. 因為 Grace 的壞脾氣，沒人想要跟她交朋友。(請用 Due to... 作答)

   _____

4. 因為 Daniel 很友善，所以他有很多朋友。(請用 Because... 作答)

   _____

5. 幸虧有 Allen 的建議，我終於解決這個危機。

   _____

I. 選擇題 (每題 5%)

(　　) 1. Max has some pen pals, some of _____ are foreigners.

　　(A) them 　　　(B) who 　　　(C) whom 　　　(D) which

(　　) 2. What Brad has to do every day is _____ good care of his five children.

　　(A) taking 　　　(B) taken 　　　(C) take 　　　(D) took

(　　) 3. _____ got lost in the mountains could hardly be found.

　　(A) Whoever 　　(B) Whenever 　　(C) Wherever 　　(D) Whichever

(　　) 4. Looking on the bright side was the only choice _____ Harry could make.

　　(A) which 　　　(B) that 　　　(C) what 　　　(D) when

(　　) 5. The thought that Ethan might know the secret really _____ me.

　　(A) shocking to 　　(B) shocked by 　　(C) shock 　　　(D) shocked

II. 填充題：請填入適當的詞，每格一字 (每題 5%)

_____ 1. I have three cars, and two of _____ are black.

_____ 2. All _____ Audrey has to do is listen to her father.

_____ 3. This is the very school _____ I went to when I lived in this area.

_____ 4. The principle is based on the idea _____ all people are created equal.

_____ 5. John asked us _____ Allen was present at the meeting or not yesterday.

III. 合併與改寫：請用適當的詞來合併與改寫句子 (每題 5%)

1. I have watched 50 movies. Most of them are action movies. (請用 ..., most... 合併)

_____

2. This is the only bus. The bus goes to the village. (請用 ...that... 合併)

_____

3. Nancy and Sam got divorced. It really surprised me. (請用 The fact... 合併)

_____

4. Who broke the vase? We had no idea about it. (請用 ...who... 合併)

_____

5. When did May leave? Leo didn't know it. (請用 ...when... 合併)

_____

IV. 整句式翻譯 (每題 5%)

1. 學生們每天所必須要做的就是認真學習、快樂生活。

_____

2. 這個蛋糕是我吃過最好吃的甜點。

_____

3. Andy 決定辭職的事讓我很震驚。(請用 The fact... 的句型作答)

_____

4. 科學家不完全明白宇宙如何運作。

_____

5. Jack 昨天沒有告訴他媽媽他會何時回家。

_____

I. 選擇題 (每題 5%)

(   ) 1. It occurred _____ me that Stanley's birthday is next month.

       (A) with   (B) of   (C) to   (D) on

(   ) 2. It is not _____ that driving fast might lead to accidents.

       (A) surprise   (B) surprising   (C) surprised   (D) to surprise

(   ) 3. It is _____ that Morris will change his mind.

       (A) like   (B) likely   (C) to like   (D) liking

(   ) 4. It came _____ no surprise that Kevin finally reached the mountain peak.

       (A) with   (B) of   (C) to   (D) as

(   ) 5. It's vital that Grace _____ all the assignments on time.

       (A) to finish   (B) is finishing   (C) finished   (D) finish

II. 填充題：請填入適當的詞或詞性變化 (as、it、dawn、occur 或 strike)，每格一字 (每題 5%)

_____ 1. It _____ on Rita that she forgot about the meeting.

_____ 2. It never _____ to me that I would fall in love with him.

_____ 3. It came _____ no surprise that one-third of the schoolchildren were overweight.

_____ 4. _____ is more likely that older people get injured easily when they exercise.

_____ 5. It _____ me that today is my dad's birthday.

III. 合併與改寫：請用適當的詞來合併與改寫句子 (每題 5%)

1. Grace never thought that she hadn't been invited to the party. (請以動詞 occur 改寫)

2. Sarah worked as a military officer, which really didn't surprise me. (請以 ...no surprise... 改寫)

_____

3. Unsurprisingly, Mike didn't attend his sister's wedding. (請以 ...surprising... 改寫)

_____

4. It is likely that Kevin will buy a new laptop. (請以 Kevin... 作為句子的開頭來改寫)

_____

5. Every driver should follow traffic rules. It is crucial. (請以 ...crucial that... 合併)

_____

IV. 整句式翻譯 (每題 5%)

1. 我在上班途中突然想到我忘記關瓦斯。

_____

2. Alex 成為一名飛行員一點也不讓人驚訝。

_____

3. Bill 很有可能在這家公司當經理。

_____

4. 有信心和決心，Jane 可能會達成目標。

_____

5. 人人守法是重要的。

_____

I. 選擇題 (每題 5%)

(　　) 1. It seemed _____ Johnny didn't like Japanese food.

　　　(A) that　　　　(B) if　　　　(C) whether　　　　(D) when

(　　) 2. Cellphones make it more convenient _____ communicate with people.

　　　(A) by　　　　(B) in　　　　(C) to　　　　(D) which

(　　) 3. _____ healthily is important for everyone.

　　　(A) Eat　　　　(B) Eating　　　　(C) Be eaten　　　　(D) To be eaten

(　　) 4. _____ has it that Bruce will drop out of school.

　　　(A) A rumor　　　　(B) The rumor　　　　(C) Rumor　　　　(D) Rumors

(　　) 5. Steve found _____ difficult to speak in public.

　　　(A) that　　　　(B) it　　　　(C) which　　　　(D) who

II. 填充題：請填入適當的詞或詞性變化，每格一字 (每題 5%)

_____ 1. The high-speed rail _____ (make) it faster to travel between Taipei and Kaohsiung.

_____ 2. It is _____ (say) that the meeting will be canceled.

_____ 3. _____ is fun for kids to fly kites in the park on weekends.

_____ 4. It's never _____ late to learn.

_____ 5. Steve seems _____ know what is wrong with Amy.

III. 合併與改寫：請用適當的詞來合併與改寫句子 (每題 5%)

1. It is easy for me to talk to foreigners in English. (請用 ...find it easy... 改寫)

_____

2. Many people think that talking to the mayor is a privilege. (請用 ...consider it a privilege... 改寫)

_____

3. People say that the superstar will retire next year. (請用 It... 改寫)

_____

4. It seems that Howard is a vegetarian. (請以 Howard... 作為句子開頭來改寫)

_____

5. The information that Mark will be the general manager of the company is a rumor. (請用 Rumor has it... 改寫)

_____

IV. 整句式翻譯 (每題 5%)

1. 捷運使人們通勤更方便。

_____

2. 謠傳 Andy 下個月要結婚。

_____

3. 這位病人太虛弱而無法行走。(請用 ...too...to... 作答)

_____

4. 均衡飲食很重要。

_____

5. Ted 在派對上似乎很高興。

_____

I. 選擇題 (每題 5%)

(   ) 1. If Tina _____ still a student, she would study harder.

      (A) were   (B) was   (C) is   (D) be

(   ) 2. If Helen _____ to study abroad, she might have broadened her horizons.

      (A) had chosen   (B) chose   (C) chooses   (D) was choosing

(   ) 3. Had it not been for the snow, I might _____ home.

      (A) have been arrived   (B) have arrived

      (C) be arrived   (D) arrived

(   ) 4. I wish that I _____ Mary a diamond ring on our wedding day last year.

      (A) gave   (B) give   (C) had given   (D) was giving

(   ) 5. It's time that he _____ home.

      (A) goes   (B) go   (C) went   (D) will go

II. 填充題：請填入適當的詞或詞性變化，每格一字 (每題 5%)

_____ 1. If Alex hadn't called, I would have _____ (forget) about the meeting.

_____ 2. If it were not for Dave's help, I could not _____ (solve) the problem.

_____ 3. We wish Jerry and Jane _____ (happy).

_____ 4. It's high time that Tina _____ (get) a job after graduation.

_____ 5. It's high time for Tom to _____ (make) his future plans.

III. 合併與改寫：請用適當的詞來合併與改寫句子 (每題 5%)

1. I am not a doctor, so I can't give you the prescription. (請用 If I... 改寫)

_____

2. If it hadn't been for the police, the murderer would still have been at large. (請用 Had it... 改寫)

_____

3. Were it not for the donations, the foundation might be shut down. (請用 If it... 改寫)

_____

4. I am not Superman, but I wish I were. (請用 I wish... 改寫)

_____

5. It's time that Andy took his parents' advice. (請用 ...to... 改寫)

_____

IV. 整句式翻譯 (每題 5%)

1. 如果我是你，我不會借錢給 Samuel。

_____

2. 如果你去年投資這家公司，你會損失很多錢。

_____

3. 如果你不是我的朋友，我就不會幫你。

_____

4. 但願我是個有名的畫家。

_____

5. 該是我們開始規劃退休的時候了。

_____

I. 選擇題 (每題 5%)

(   ) 1. Joe never ate without _____ a drink.

    (A) have   (B) having   (C) has   (D) had

(   ) 2. Amy did not come _____ telling me in advance.

    (A) but   (B) and   (C) without   (D) with

(   ) 3. No one can deny _____ hard work is a key to success.

    (A) that   (B) if   (C) when   (D) what

(   ) 4. We can never take it too _____ when it comes to pursuing life goals.

    (A) serious   (B) seriously enough

    (C) seriously   (D) enough serious

(   ) 5. Terry can afford to buy a plane, _____ a car.

    (A) not to mention   (B) let alone   (C) much less   (D) not to say of

II. 填充題：請填入適當的詞或詞性變化 (no、too、without 或 enough)，每格一字 (每題 5%)

_____ 1. Alex never calls me _____ telling me a joke.

_____ 2. There is _____ denying that Taipei 101 is a popular tourist attraction.

_____ 3. People can't be _____ nice when getting along with others.

_____ 4. We can't be generous _____ in helping the poor.

_____ 5. My high school life would not be complete _____ a graduation trip.

III. 合併與改寫：請用適當的詞來合併與改寫句子 (每題 5%)

1. Every time when Tina goes window-shopping, she always buys a new pair of shoes. (請用 ...not...without... 改寫)

   _____

2. It can't be denied that Jay is a world-famous singer. (請用 There... 改寫)

   _____

3. We can never thank him too gratefully when it comes to his hard work. (請用 ...enough... 改寫)

   _____

4. Students can never study too hard when preparing for the final exam. (請用 ...enough... 改寫)

   _____

5. Steve can't ride a bike, not to speak of riding a motorcycle. (請用 ...much less... 改寫)

   _____

IV. 整句式翻譯 (每題 5%)

1. Jennifer 每次來臺灣都來探望我。(請用 ...without... 作答)

   _____

2. 無可否認的，Matt 是個電腦奇才 (wizard)。

   _____

3. 我們處理化學製品時，再怎麼小心也不為過。

   _____

4. 在開車這方面我們再謹慎也不為過。

   _____

5. 這位獵人能夠獵鹿，更不用說兔子了。

   _____

I. 選擇題 (每題 5%)

( ) 1. Rarely _____ eat seafood because she is allergic to it.

    (A) does Sarah   (B) was Sarah   (C) Sarah does   (D) Sarah was

( ) 2. 下列句子何者正確？

    (A) Here the bus comes.   (B) Here comes it.

    (C) Here should they come.   (D) Here you are.

( ) 3. Seldom _____ stay out late.

    (A) David is   (B) David was   (C) does David   (D) is David

( ) 4. Only when you are a father _____ you realize how difficult it is to raise children.

    (A) do   (B) did   (C) will   (D) would

( ) 5. _____ a good driver Louis is!

    (A) How   (B) What   (C) When   (D) Where

II. 填充題：請填入適當的詞或詞性變化，每格一字 (每題 5%)

_____ 1. Hardly _____ we know each other although we were once classmates.

_____ 2. Not only _____ Harry like dogs but he also loves cats.

_____ 3. On the main road _____ (be) the convenient store.

_____ 4. Cathy went home only _____ find that she lost her keys.

_____ 5. _____ a charming man Daniel is!

III. 合併與改寫：請用適當的詞來合併與改寫句子 (每題 5%)

1. Jasmine seldom went to the movies at night. (請用 Seldom... 改寫)

2. Wendy didn't come home until the rain stopped. (請用 Not until... 改寫)

_____

3. The bird stood on a branch. (請用 On... 改寫)

_____

4. Hazel would see a show only if she got a free ticket. (請用 Only if... 改寫)

_____

5. How beautiful the girl is! (請用 What... 改寫)

_____

IV. 整句式翻譯 (每題 5%)

1. 鄰居們都不太知道火災的原因。(請用 Little... 作答)

_____

2. Jane 從未忘記她父母教導的事物。(請用 Never... 作答)

_____

3. 郵局位於餐廳旁。(請用 Beside... 作答)

_____

4. 只有當你失去某樣事物時，你才會珍惜你所擁有的。(請用 Only when... 作答)

_____

5. Tommy 多麼聰明啊！(請用 How... 作答)

_____

I. 選擇題 (每題 5%)

( ) 1. It was in the train _____ Dave met his girlfriend.

(A) what   (B) which   (C) that   (D) when

( ) 2. Not until this month _____ he released from prison.

(A) did   (B) does   (C) could   (D) was

( ) 3. Not until last night _____ Steve hand in his report.

(A) was   (B) did   (C) does   (D) will

( ) 4. The ceremony didn't come to an end _____ midnight.

(A) until   (B) with   (C) of   (D) within

( ) 5. 下列何者為 2/7 之正確表達法？

(A) two-sevens   (B) two-sevenths

(C) second-sevenths   (D) second-seven

II. 填充題：請填入適當的詞或詞性變化，每格一字 (每題 5%)

_____ 1. It was on the bus _____ the children are talking loudly.

_____ 2. Not until Frank reached the mountaintop _____ he realize how far he had come.

_____ 3. It was not until last summer _____ they saw each other again.

_____ 4. 2/5 = two out of _____

_____ 5. 3/100 = three _____ one hundred

III. 合併與改寫：請用適當的詞來合併與改寫句子 (每題 5%)

1. Mike was taking a nap in the living room. (請用 It...that... 改寫，標底線處為要強調的部分)

_____

2. Sandra was playing frisbee in the park. (請用 It...that... 改寫，標底線處為要強調的部分)

_____

3. It was not until 3 a.m. yesterday that Lily finished her report. (請用 ...not...until... 改寫)

_____

4. Joseph didn't tell the truth until his father came. (請用 It was not until... 改寫)

_____

5. The police didn't arrest the criminal until four years later. (請用 Not until... 改寫)

_____

IV. 整句式翻譯 (每題 5%)

1. 得到歌唱比賽第一名的正是 Richard Yang。(請用 It... 作答)

_____

2. 你完成你的作業之後才能出去外面玩。(請用 Not until... 作答)

_____

3. 贏得最佳女主角獎的正是 Jennifer。(請用 It... 作答)

_____

4. 在臺灣超過三分之一的中學生近視。

_____

5. 這所學校每二十個學生當中有三個來自單親家庭。

_____

Answer Key

第1回

I. 選擇題

1. C　2. A　3. D　4. B　5. A

II. 填充題

1. closed　2. happy　3. cost　4. stolen

5. riding

III. 合併與改寫

1. I spent NT$1,500 buying the watch.

　= I spent NT$1,500 on the watch.

2. It tastes delicious.

3. I saw Grace running in the park.

4. It takes me 30 minutes to do my homework

　every day.

5. I found Eric crying in the room.

IV. 整句式翻譯

1. Alex always stays/keeps calm when he runs

　into trouble.

2. I heard Mary chatting/chat with her brother in

　the next room.

3. The typhoon left hundreds of people

　homeless.

4. I spend 50 minutes watching TV news every

　day.

　= I spend 50 minutes on TV news every day.

5. The new book cost me NT$500.

　= It cost me NT$500 to buy the new book.

第2回

I. 選擇題

1. A　2. B　3. B　4. D　5. D

II. 填充題

1. sell　2. open　3. go　4. drink　5. as

III. 合併與改寫

1. Sarah could not help buying her brother a new

　computer.

　= Sarah could not help but buy her brother a

　new computer.

2. Brad used to play tennis in the evening.

3. I prefer tea to coffee.

4. Nancy prefers to watch TV at home rather

　than go window-shopping.

5. I regard Mary as a hard-working person.

IV. 整句式翻譯

1. A lot of people see/view/regard/think of/look

　(up)on Will as a good pitcher.

2. Nancy prefers walking to driving.

　= Nancy prefers to walk rather than drive.

　= Nancy would rather walk than drive.

3. Allen used to eat rice for breakfast.

4. George is not used to the heavy traffic in

　Taipei.

5. Rick could not help crying when he saw the

　lonely old man.

　= Rick could not help but cry when he saw the

　lonely old man.

第3回

I. 選擇題

1. B　2. A　3. C　4. C　5. C

II. 填充題

1. of   2. of   3. located/situated   4. occurred
5. to

III. 合併與改寫

1. We informed Tom of the good news.
2. The basketball team consists of ten players.
3. The post office is situated behind the tall building.
4. The diamond ring belongs to Miss Lin.
5. A big celebration takes place every year to honor the war heroes.

IV. 整句式翻譯

1. Richard was deprived of the right to vote.
2. The robber robbed Amy of her necklace.
3. Our class is made up of 20 students.
   = Our class consists of 20 students.
   = Our class comprises 20 students.
   = Our class is composed/comprised of 20 students.
4. The restaurant sits/lies/stands on the busy street.
   = The restaurant is located/situated on the busy street.
5. The school's anniversary celebration takes place in November every year.

第 4 回

I. 選擇題

1. D   2. C   3. C   4. B   5. A

II. 填充題

1. for   2. been   3. have   4. take   5. fail

III. 合併與改寫

1. I have been busy since yesterday.
2. By the time I arrived at the station, the train had left.
3. Daniel should have got up early this morning.
4. Ann insisted that her son (should) go to bed before 10 p.m.
5. Fred behaved himself for fear of being punished.

IV. 整句式翻譯

1. In recent years, smartphones have been very popular.
2. By the time I got home, Mom had left.
3. My wallet must be in my book bag.
4. The teacher recommended that Miranda (should) apply to graduate school.
5. Jenny took a taxi to work for fear of being late.
   = Jenny took a taxi to work for fear that she would/might be late.
   = Jenny took a taxi to work lest she (should) be late.

第 5 回

I. 選擇題

1. A   2. B   3. C   4. A   5. A

II. 填充題

1. order　2. Practicing　3. Failing

4. communicating　5. Exercise

III. 合併與改寫

1. David walks to work with an eye to saving money.

2. Getting good grades really made Leo happy.

3. Alex had difficulty running a marathon in under four hours.

4. Tens of thousands of people gathered in Times Square so that they could celebrate the New Year.

5. Asked a personal question, Dennis felt unhappy.

IV. 整句式翻譯

1. Andy works hard to/in order to support his family.

   = Andy works hard so as to support his family.

   = Andy works hard with a view to/with an eye to supporting his family.

   = Andy works hard in order that/so that he can support his family.

2. Not getting home before 10 p.m., Rick was scolded by his father.

3. Jeff had trouble/difficulty/a hard time/problems falling asleep, so he decided to see a doctor.

4. Do you mind lending me your new book?

   = Do you mind lending your new book to me?

5. Going to bed early and waking up early is a good habit.

= Keeping early hours is a good habit.

第 6 回

I. 選擇題

1. B　2. B　3. B　4. C　5. C

II. 填充題

1. inclusive　2. shaking　3. being　4. sold

5. Practicing

III. 合併與改寫

1. Five people bought the TV set at a lower price, including Andy.

2. Daniel took a rest on the sofa with his legs crossed.

3. Scolded by his parents, William was in a bad mood.

4. There are five students riding their bikes in the park.

5. Saving the drowning boy, James was praised by the mayor.

IV. 整句式翻譯

1. Jacob recommended ten candidates, including/inclusive of Grace.

   = Jacob recommended ten candidates, Grace included.

2. Getting stuck in a traffic jam, Charlotte was late for work.

3. There were ten students selected to participate in the graduate program.

4. Not knowing what to do, Mia left without saying a word.

5. Paul was shocked at the news, with his hands trembling.

第 7 回

I. 選擇題

1. C   2. C   3. C   4. D   5. B

II. 填充題

1. the   2. with   3. other   4. others

5. anything

III. 合併與改寫

1. The mood really has a lot to do with the weather.

2. Mike's performance had nothing to do with the job training.

3. One of his (three) flowers is purple, another is red, and the other is yellow.

4. One of my (two) dogs is black, and the other is white.

5. There is something surprising happening.

IV. 整句式翻譯

1. Adam's failure had something to do with bad luck.

2. One of Alex's twin sisters is a doctor; the other is a bus driver.

   = One of Alex's twin sisters is a doctor, and the other is a bus driver.

3. Jenny's good temper has a lot/much to do with the education she received.

4. Some people prefer noodles, while others prefer rice.

5. Is there anything special today?

第 8 回

I. 選擇題

1. A   2. D   3. C   4. D   5. C

II. 填充題

1. of   2. delight   3. cheaper   4. more

5. astonishment

III. 合併與改寫

1. Mom had nothing of value.

2. To my surprise, Dave lost the game.

3. Evelyn is much shorter than Iris.

   = Iris is much taller than Evelyn.

4. Exercise is of great importance to everyone.

5. To the teacher's disappointment, his students didn't listen to him.

IV. 整句式翻譯

1. The watch was of great significance to David.

2. To Gary's regret, he dropped out of high school.

3. Ian wrote his letters more carefully than most of us.

4. Hugo is a lot/much/far older than Jerry.

5. To our shock, the minister was involved in the scandal.

第 9 回

I. 選擇題

1. C   2. D   3. A   4. C   5. B

II. 填充題

1. more　2. longer　3. much　4. hard
5. possible

III. 合併與改寫

1. The better you sleep, the healthier you will become.
2. Your car is three times more expensive than mine.
3. Wayne is as old as Lucy.
4. Margaret has as many cars as Nina.
5. Phoebe came home as early as she could.

IV. 整句式翻譯

1. The more Hazel thought, the more anxious she became.
2. The less you want, the more easily you will be satisfied.
3. My hair is three times longer than yours.
   = My hair is three times as long as yours.
   = My hair is three times the length of yours.
4. I have as many pens as you (do).
5. Craig made his plans as carefully as possible.
   = Craig made his plans as carefully as he could.

第 10 回

I. 選擇題

1. C　2. C　3. B　4. A　5. C

II. 填充題

1. to　2. as　3. in　4. to　5. of

III. 合併與改寫

1. Tom is looking forward to seeing his girlfriend soon.
2. Francis is famous for his acting.
3. Jennifer was immersed in studying English.
4. Bob stayed home helping his mom clean the house instead of going window-shopping.
5. The heavy rain led to flooding.

IV. 整句式翻譯

1. Anne devoted herself to helping the poor.
2. I will prevent Brian from making the same mistake.
3. Unfortunately, he was addicted to drugs.
4. Joe wanted to play basketball instead of/rather than sleeping at home.
   = Instead of/Rather than sleeping at home, Joe wanted to play basketball.
5. Kevin is famous as an excellent lawyer.

第 11 回

I. 選擇題

1. B　2. B　3. A　4. C　5. B

II. 填充題

1. did　2. neither　3. so　4. needs　5. is

III. 合併與改寫

1. Nick doesn't like Korean food, and neither does Oscar.
2. Eat healthy and light food, or you will get sick easily.

3. Both Daniel and Peter work in the factory.

4. Sean not only ate a hamburger but also drank a cup of coffee for breakfast.

5. As soon as Victor walked into the living room, he turned on the air conditioner.

IV. 整句式翻譯

1. I don't understand French, and neither/nor does Lisa.

2. Obey/Follow the traffic rules, or you will get a ticket.

3. You can't go out to play unless you finish your homework.

4. Neither Darcy nor Gilbert is an engineer.

5. As soon as/The moment/The minute/The instant I left my house, it started to rain.

= No sooner had I left my house than it started to rain.

第 12 回

I. 選擇題

1. C   2. A   3. B   4. A   5. A

II. 填充題

1. such   2. whether   3. as   4. that   5. such

III. 合併與改寫

1. Difficult as the task is, I still want to overcome it.

2. In spite of knowing it was dangerous, Steve still dived into the water to save his brother.

3. Tina put a lot of effort into her work so that she could get a pay rise.

4. Nancy is such a reliable person that she has won her customers' confidence.

5. Although Johnny lacked money, he set up his own company without delay.

IV. 整句式翻譯

1. It doesn't matter whether/if Edward stays here or not.

2. Katie attended/participated in/took part in the speech contest so that she might win the cash prize.

3. Daniel is such a kind person that everyone wants to make friends with him.

4. Although/Though David did not earn/make much money, he led a happy life.

= Despite/In spite of the fact that he did not earn/make much money, David led a happy life.

= Despite/In spite of not earning/making much money, David led a happy life.

5. Fat as the cat looks, it runs fast.

第 13 回

I. 選擇題

1. B   2. C   3. D   4. A   5. C

II. 填充題

1. While   2. of   3. because/since   4. because

5. because/since

III. 合併與改寫

1. John got promoted because of his hard work.

2. Some people don't like stinky tofu while some

(people) enjoy it.

3. We can't play basketball because it is raining hard outside.

4. While Jason didn't get good grades, he still didn't give up and worked hard.

5. Johnny was watching a football game while Jimmy was sleeping in his room.

IV. 整句式翻譯

1. While I have been working with Wayne for 20 years, I still do not understand him.

2. Some students like art while others like natural science.

3. Due to Grace's bad temper, no one wants to be friends with her.

4. Because Daniel is friendly, he has many/lots of/a lot of friends.

5. Thanks to Allen's advice/suggestion, I finally resolved the crisis.

第 14 回

I. 選擇題

1. C   2. C   3. A   4. B   5. D

II. 填充題

1. them   2. that   3. that   4. that
5. whether/if

III. 合併與改寫

1. I have watched 50 movies, most of which are action movies.

2. This is the only bus that goes to the village.

3. The fact that Nancy and Sam got divorced

really surprised me.

4. We had no idea about who broke the vase.

5. Leo didn't know when May left.

IV. 整句式翻譯

1. What/All (that) the students have to do every day is study hard and live happily.

2. This cake is the most delicious dessert that I have ever had/eaten/tasted.

3. The fact that Andy decided to resign shocked me.

4. Scientists do not fully understand how the universe works.

5. Jack didn't tell his mother when he would come home yesterday.

第 15 回

I. 選擇題

1. C   2. B   3. B   4. D   5. D

II. 填充題

1. dawned   2. occurred   3. as   4. It
5. struck

III. 合併與改寫

1. It never occurred to Grace that she hadn't been invited to the party.

2. It came as no surprise that Sarah worked as a military officer.

3. It was not surprising that Mike didn't attend his sister's wedding.

4. Kevin is likely to buy a new laptop.

5. It is crucial that every driver (should) follow

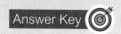

traffic rules.

IV. 整句式翻譯

1. It occurred to me on the way to work that I forgot to turn off the gas.

   = It struck me on the way to work that I forgot to turn off the gas.

   = It dawned on me on the way to work that I forgot to turn off the gas.

2. It was not surprising that Alex became a pilot.

   = It came as no surprise that Alex became a pilot.

   = Unsurprisingly, Alex became a pilot.

3. It is likely that Bill <u>works/is working</u> as a manager in the company.

   = Bill is likely to work as a manager in the company.

4. With confidence and determination, Jane is likely to achieve the goal.

5. It is <u>vital/critical/crucial/important/essential/necessary</u> that everyone (should) obey the law.

第 16 回

I. 選擇題

1. A   2. C   3. B   4. C   5. B

II. 填充題

1. makes   2. said   3. It   4. too   5. to

III. 合併與改寫

1. I find it easy to talk to foreigners in English.

2. Many people consider it a privilege to talk to the mayor.

3. It is said that the superstar will retire next year.

4. Howard seems to be a vegetarian.

5. Rumor has it that Mark will be the general manager of the company.

IV. 整句式翻譯

1. The MRT makes it more convenient for people to commute.

2. Rumor has it that Andy will get married next month.

3. The patient is too weak to walk.

4. It is important to have a balanced diet.

   = Having a balanced diet is important.

   = To have a balanced diet is important.

5. It seemed that Ted was happy at the party.

   = Ted seemed to be happy at the party.

第 17 回

I. 選擇題

1. A   2. A   3. B   4. C   5. C

II. 填充題

1. forgotten   2. solve   3. happiness   4. got
5. make

III. 合併與改寫

1. If I were a doctor, I could give you the prescription.

2. Had it not been for the police, the murderer would still have been at large.

3. If it were not for the donations, the foundation might be shut down.

4. I wish I were Superman.

5. It's time for Andy to take his parents' advice.

IV. 整句式翻譯

1. If I were you, I wouldn't lend Samuel money.

2. If you had invested in the company last year, you might have lost a lot of money.

3. If you were not my friend, I would not help you.

4. I wish I were a famous painter.

5. It's time that we started planning for retirement.

   = It's time for us to start planning for retirement.

第18回

I. 選擇題

1. B　2. C　3. A　4. C　5. A

II. 填充題

1. without　2. no　3. too　4. enough

5. without

III. 合併與改寫

1. Tina does not go window-shopping without buying a new pair of shoes.

2. There is no denying that Jay is a world-famous singer.

3. We can never thank him gratefully enough when it comes to his hard work.

4. Students can never study hard enough when preparing for the final exam.

5. Steve can't ride a bike, much less ride a

motorcycle.

IV. 整句式翻譯

1. Jennifer never comes to Taiwan without visiting me.

   = Jennifer doesn't come to Taiwan without visiting me.

2. No one can deny that Matt is a computer wizard.

   = It can't be denied that Matt is a computer wizard.

   = There is no denying that Matt is a computer wizard.

3. We can never/cannot/can't be too careful when handling chemicals.

   = We can never/cannot/can't be careful enough when handling chemicals.

4. We can never/cannot/can't be too cautious in driving.

   = We can never/cannot/can't be cautious enough in driving.

5. The hunter could hunt a deer, not to mention/ not to speak of/to say nothing of a rabbit.

第19回

I. 選擇題

1. A　2. D　3. C　4. C　5. B

II. 填充題

1. did/do　2. does　3. is/was　4. to

5. What

III. 合併與改寫

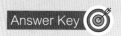

1. Seldom did Jasmine go to the movies at night.

2. Not until the rain stopped did Wendy come home.

3. On a branch stood the bird.

4. Only if Hazel got a free ticket would she see a show.

5. What a beautiful girl (she is)!

IV. 整句式翻譯

1. Little did the neighbors know the cause of the fire.

2. Never did Jane forget what her parents taught her.

3. Beside the restaurant is/lies/stands/sits the post office.

4. Only when you lose something will you cherish what you have.

5. How smart Tommy is!

第 20 回

I. 選擇題

1. C   2. D   3. B   4. A   5. B

II. 填充題

1. that   2. did   3. that   4. five   5. over

III. 合併與改寫

1. It was Mike that was taking a nap in the living room.

2. It was in the park that Sandra was playing frisbee.

3. Lily did not finish her report until 3 a.m. yesterday.

4. It was not until Joseph's father came that he told the truth.

5. Not until four years later did the police arrest the criminal.

IV. 整句式翻譯

1. It was Richard Yang that won first place in the singing contest.

2. Not until you have finished your homework can you go out and play.

3. It was Jennifer that won the best actress award.

4. Over one-third of high school students in Taiwan are nearsighted.

5. Three out of twenty students at this school are from single-parent families.

英文歷屆學測超絕剖析 & 模擬實戰
英文歷屆指考超絕剖析 & 模擬實戰

‧囊括近八年試題，讓你熟悉題型、穩握趨勢。

‧收錄四回模擬實戰，全真模擬大考試題，讓你身歷其境、累積經驗。

‧詳盡試題剖析，逐題詳解有如名師在陣。

‧詳解本獨立成冊，參照方便，省時有效率。

配合全書章節分類編排，複習句型一本搞定！

共 20 回，每回 4 大題，精選 4 大題型：

選擇題、填充題、合併與改寫、整句式翻譯，

每題型各有 5 小題，精準、迅速、效率滿分！